Praise for *A New Climate for Christology*

"The late Sallie McFague left us with yet one more amazing gift. In her usual inimitable, clear, and compelling prose, McFague offers Christians a response to the existential threat that climate change poses to our planet and all of its inhabitants. Science and theology share a common story, she demonstrates: that all of creation is relational and interdependent—in life and death. Dying gives rise to new life—at every level—and embodies the self-emptying love of the Trinitarian God. May we follow her exhortation to embrace our place in the cycle of life and love so that this vibrant world may flourish."

—Ellen T. Armour, associate dean of academic affairs;
E. Rhodes and Leona B. Carpenter Associate Professor of
Feminist Theology; director, Carpenter Program in Religion,
Gender, and Sexuality, Vanderbilt Divinity School

"Sallie McFague—¡Presente! While she may no longer be with us, her words and her wisdom continue to challenge us in this posthumous book. Moving beyond the misused story of sinners before an angry God, McFague invites us to a relational dance with creation and divinity as the means of finding salvation not just for humanity, but also for our planet. Failure to live into this kenosis calling condemns us and the earth we occupy. The insightful challenge McFague gives in *A New Climate for Christology* demands our full consideration."

—Miguel De La Torre, professor of social ethics and
Latinx studies, Iliff School of Theology

D1595766

A New Climate for Christology

A New Climate for Christology

Kenosis, Climate Change, and Befriending Nature

Sallie McFague

Fortress Press
Minneapolis

A NEW CLIMATE FOR CHRISTOLOGY
Kenosis, Climate Change, and Befriending Nature

Cover image: iStock 2021: Idyllic forest glade mossy woodland by fotoVoyager
Cover design: Joe Reinke

Print ISBN: 978-1-5064-7873-9
eBook ISBN: 978-1-5064-7874-6

Contents

Publisher's Note

Over the course of more than forty years, Sallie McFague published eight major volumes with Fortress Press, building in that time a rich legacy of thought that has challenged and changed generations of readers. Thus it is a special privilege to bring to the public *A New Climate for Christology*, the final manuscript Sallie completed before her death.

We are grateful for the support that Sallie's family gave to this project and to Ashley John Moyse for his assistance.

Prologue

Jesus Christ and Climate Change

Our planet is certainly at one of its crucial "turning points." Unless we wake up, spurn denial, and ready ourselves for serious kenotic (sacrificial) action, life on our planet will deteriorate at both human and other life-form levels. Human action is determined in part by the picture, the story, of our lives. Where we fit into "the scheme of things" is important because our actions are influenced by our beliefs. As Annie Dillard says, "We wake up, if we wake at all, to mystery, rumors of death, beauty, violence. . . . 'Seem like we're just down here,' a woman said to me recently, 'and don't nobody know why.'"[1]

The answer to the question of why we are here makes all the difference in how we live on planet earth. For several hundred years now, Western human beings have explained that mystery with a story in which we are at the top of the planetary scale, where the purpose of all other life-forms is to service and benefit us. It is a utilitarian, hierarchical worldview in which we are the only subjects and everything and everybody else is an "object" for our use. This picture has resulted in a lonely, dead world as our "home" and a deteriorating, lifeless world as everyone else's "home." Moreover, the future looks grim for everyone—human beings and the billions of creatures who serve us. This worldview as evident in one of its results—rampant, unregulated capitalism—has been tried, and it has failed.

We need a new story about who we are in the scheme of things. Such stories are the work of the world's religions, and Christianity, especially kenotic Christianity, has an attractive, powerful story to offer. The present book is an attempt to sketch the main features of this candidate. Its principal feature—as is true of many religions—is a countercultural call to human beings to live "for others" as the only possible response in a world that is characterized by giving and receiving, symbiosis and sharing, reciprocal interdependence, life and death. What we see in evolution, a system of radical and total interdependence, is mirrored at all levels of planetary action, up to and including examples of self-sacrificial (kenotic) activity of some human beings that other life-forms may flourish. A grain of wheat does not fulfill its destiny until it dies in order to provide food for others. Self-sacrificial, altruistic action is in continuity with that grain of wheat, although at the human level, it must be a self-conscious decision as the way to live.

Hence what the religions have to offer are ways for human beings, the only self-conscious actors on the planet, to live in such a way that *all* might flourish. The picture of reality that the religions offer is not a spiritual, otherworldly one but a picture for living justly and fruitfully on this planet. Christianity underscores this perspective by its claim of incarnationalism—God present here and now. Hence most religions are not recommending ways to escape the pain of life on planet earth, but on the contrary, they are telling us that the *only* way to live well on this planet is by following its "house rules": (1) take only your share, (2) clean up after yourself, (3) keep the house in good repair for future occupants. As obvious as these "rules" may sound, even fulfilling the first one implies something like the "Golden Rule," which is a serious challenge for most of us.

However, Trinitarian Christianity and nature share a common characteristic—intrinsic relationality. At the quantum level, relationality is more basic than existence (substances): "I relate; therefore I am." Trinitarianism says likewise: the activity of love among the "persons" of the Trinity means divine relationality is central. The evolutionary perspective is intrinsically protoaltruistic, displaying features such as give-and-take, sharing, symbiosis, and life and death. So at both the level of nature and the level of the essence of God (the Trinity), relationality is basic and central. It is impossible for an individual to exist alone. Hence our status is relational all the way down and up and in every way. Trinitarianism and nature are both radically relational.

Evolution claims that a grain of wheat does not nourish unless it dies, and the Trinity says that divine life (and love) is the dance of giving and receiving among the "persons" of the Trinity. All life and love (reality) is characterized by this pattern of neediness and giving/receiving; hence the fundamental posture of its self-conscious life-form (the human being) is one of daily radical gratitude. So "faith" is the willingness to lead a totally intradependent, receiving life from God and others, as well as passing that life along. In this paradigm, there is no stopping place where one "owns" or possesses oneself: the movement is a constant receiving life from others and passing it along. Hence what is practiced at the evolutionary level is a faint shadow of the only true life—a pattern of giving and receiving, but with the receiving more basic and coming first. We can give because we have received everything: our very life and all that we care about.

I want to think through the problem of how views of Christian salvation contribute to or hinder our crisis with climate change. Is there any relation between the way we think and the way we act? Especially I want to look at a kenotic interpretation of Christianity: the odd arrangement whereby in order to gain your life, you must lose it. The way of the cross is total self-emptying so that one can receive life, real life, and then pass this life on. Life is never to be possessed (the Christian understanding of sin). Most of creation abides by this rule through evolution—dying that new life might occur. It is a constant, continuous process of receiving and giving, in an unending circle of give-and-take. One sees it initially in the life and death cycles of evolution, and one sees it in the kenotic pattern of the Trinity: even God is this loving activity, not a "being" of any sort.

If one accepts this interpretation, then we human beings have to give over to this process and believe in its power and its results. There is no certainty, so why would anyone choose it? This interpretation says there is no alternative—we wish there were, and we struggle hard to believe in any strategy that does have certainty and that we can "possess." We do not want to be à la Søren Kierkegaard out over the water with no life support. Why is this so attractive? Why does it seem like such a privilege to be invited into this life? It is not a comfortable, certain life. It is living on the edge of a life raft (a small one)! But what if the only life is God's kenotic life?

The sequence of our argument begins with the introduction, with an overview of the thesis—how, with the help of some insights from postmodern philosophy, the kenotic story of Jesus (and God) is a fitting instrument for helping us react positively to the "turning point" presented by climate change. In the first chapter, we will attempt an in-depth treatment of the kenotic story of Christianity for the purposes of responding appropriately to climate change. In the second chapter, we will do a similarly expansive treatment of the contributions of postmodernism for dealing in an effective way with climate change, while in the third chapter, we will bring together the findings of the Christian kenotic story and the insights from postmodernism as contributions to a new worldview—"relational ontology." In the fourth chapter, we will attempt putting "relational ontology" into practice through three avenues, the model of friend and the theologies of Arthur C. McGill and Richard Kearney. In the fifth chapter, we will make some concluding comments on postmodern insights for climate change, the human role in climate change, and finally God's role as "hope."

In closing this prologue, I want to mention that the book does not progress in a totally linear fashion, due in part to the nature of the topic—its extreme difficulty, novelty to most of us, and complexity. I have found that repeating some material, approaching it from different angles, and being willing to allow for some "ragged edges" in the argument are essential given the challenge of relating evolution, kenotic Christianity, and climate change. As a theologian, I am not an expert in the worldview that postmodern science is presenting to us. My only claim is that if we were to embody the postmodern picture and Christian faith with the same thoroughness that we incarnate radical individualism (from the eighteenth century) into our lives, including our faith traditions, we would make a serious move in dealing with one of our greatest "turning points"—climate change. Admittedly, I am going for the "big picture," believing that as a theologian, it is the form of the scientific worldview that I need to work with. It is important that the picture I work with be the agreed-upon one of our time—that it be both generally correct and not the product of another time. Human-induced climate change is a twenty-first-century phenomenon and needs the picture of reality operative in this time.

Introduction

Kenosis, Christ, and Climate Change

I believe there is a basic story that subconsciously or unconsciously dictates many of our actions. We humans love stories. We love them because our lives are stories—we are stories. Our lives have a beginning, middle, and end, and during the time of our story, we try to see meaning in it. Who are we in our story, and what should we be doing?

In a recent book titled *Sapiens: A Brief History of Humankind*, the author, Yuval Noah Harari, informs us that for large groups of humans (beyond 150 people) to act together in light of a goal, a fiction or story is necessary. The story is what people fight—and even die—for. It is very hard to tell a good story, "yet when it succeeds, it gives human beings immense power, because it enables millions of strangers to cooperate and work towards common goals. Just try to imagine how difficult it would have been to create states, or churches, or legal systems if we could only speak about things that really exist, such as rivers, trees, and lions."[1] Thus with what Harari calls the cognitive revolution, human beings live in two "realities," with the imagined reality the more powerful of the two.

1

The Western story, anchored by a monarchical, all-powerful God, is no longer functioning to give meaning to people's lives. In a popular version of this story, Christians have had a narrative of a supernatural God telling them how to behave, and when they fail, he pays the price for their sins so that they can have eternal life in heaven. However, this religious story is no longer credible in contemporary culture. A story is most effective when it aligns the religious dimension with the secular: when they are mutually reciprocal and supportive. When the distance between the two interpretations becomes too great, the link between them breaks, and people are left adhering to just one or to none at all. The latter stance is scarcely credible, and folks will fight to hold on to their story, even an "incredible" or mediocre one, rather than be bereft of any story. Human life *must* have meaning at all costs. The Western, Christian model of God and the world is losing credibility in most quarters. It can be "patched up" only so many times, and then it doesn't "work" any longer.

However, this does not mean that all stories are useless. For instance, when folks say that they no longer "believe in God," it may mean not that they don't believe in any God but that the Western, supernatural picture of God as the all-powerful creator and controller of earthly life no longer works for them. It doesn't necessarily mean that *no* interpretation would work for them.

We need a new basic model, paradigm, of the relationship of God and the world. Currently, in most Protestant circles, the prime model is not of God and the world but of God and the human being, specifically the male human being. While Roman Catholicism has had a doctrine of the world, since the Reformation, the Protestant focus has been narrowed to human individuals, a divine and a human one. This

INTRODUCTION

picture of two beings only marginally related, very independent, highly anthropocentric, is all about *who* has the power. It is a competitive model of two isolated monads, each vying for the gold medal, as in sports. The supposition is that God can intervene on the behalf of individual human beings for their good (or not). At its most crude, the model is two competitive human beings (males) vying for controlling power.

Therefore, *power* is the heart of the issue. Who has the most? The model we choose makes all the difference. But where do we get our models? The individualistic model is a combination of Enlightenment philosophy and anthropology and market capitalism. However, Christians believe Jesus is "the face of God"; Jesus's life and death and teachings are reflections of the "ways of God." A very different model emerges from this source—what can be called the "kenotic" model. Why accept one or the other? It is a jump, a leap of faith. There is no hard and fast evidence that one is better than the other. In terms of one's most basic, deepest commitment, one cannot be certain. The test (and it is only a test, not a certainty) is that one is "better" for oneself, the planet, and other creatures. Hence Christians start with the story of Jesus. We move from there to talking about God and the world. We understand who God is (God's transcendence and immanence) and who we are because of Jesus. Does this mean literalism? Does it mean that Jesus is God and therefore we know what we Christians say is the "truth," that we need nothing else than the story of Jesus to say both who God is and who we are? No, but we do get some clear clues and directions from that story.

A kenotic theology is a story of self-sacrificing love, a model that upends the Enlightenment at its most vulnerable place. It is contrary to all we as Westerners value, expect, reward, and honor. But what if the cross (dying to one's old

3

life, trying to live a new, self-sacrificing love) *is* the way? What if we choose this as our model? How should we conceive of the transcendence/immanence of God and God's relation to the world if we take the life, death, and resurrection of Jesus as our model in a time of climate change? And what if some of the insights coming to us from postmodernism—especially its anthropology, its understanding of how we fit into the scheme of things—have some interesting overlaps with the Christian kenotic picture? What if some of the novel insights into this basic "worldview"—that is, the assumed, underlying assumptions about the human place in the world on issues of power, exceptionalism, responsibility, body, materialism, dependence, and so on—give us a very different picture than the traditional Protestant picture of two superbeings, God and man, struggling for dominance? What if we might learn something about how to live a kenotic life from the very different picture of our place on our planet from an anthropology challenging us to face up to our radical dependence, fragility, and even weakness? The seeming absurdity of living a life of sacrificial love for others that is at the heart of most religions, and certainly of Christianity, may find a partner in insights from postmodern science and philosophy in terms of its insistence that primarily and centrally, we are animals, bodies dependent on other bodies, incarnational beings at the mercy of the many sources of power in our planet—among them, climate change. The focus on the body at the heart of the Christian story of the incarnation of God should make this tradition open to some of the distinctive insights of postmodernism: its profound materialism; its suspicion of "spirit"; its call for a biocracy (in which all life-forms have a vote, unlike a democracy); its focus on human responsibility for our own actions; the call to love *this* world, not another; the insistence that we learn to face despair and death; the end of thinking in terms of "substance"; its claim that agency (subjecthood) is not limited to human beings; and so on.

So to return to our present dilemma, we might wish we could believe in an all-powerful, supernatural God who could solve all our problems, but that no longer is a persuasive argument. Why is the picture of this God no longer credible, no longer powerful? In part, it is because we no longer believe in ourselves as powerful individuals. Our whole picture of who we are and who God is has changed, so say the postmoderns. The individualistic, solitary, isolated human being who was a product of Enlightenment philosophy and Newtonian science has been undermined and with it belief in a similar picture of God. The pictures we have of ourselves and of God go together, and both have been undermined in the late twentieth and into the twenty-first centuries. Let us look at what has happened to the happy picture of progress in the latter part of the nineteenth century at the hands of the three masters of suspicion: Freud, Darwin, and Nietzsche.

These folks undermined the sense of discovery, progress, and human control during that century. The Industrial Revolution, the colonization of Africa and the East by Western powers, and advances in medicine and the other sciences combined to make human beings feel confident and, for the first time, in control of nature. This was to be short lived, however. Freud destroyed the sense of clarity that people used to feel about their "insides," their motives and desires. Until Freud, things seemed relatively straightforward, but he opened up a vast internal swampy jungle, sowing seeds of doubt, mistrust, and deceit even in our most intimate secretive selves—our relations with parents and sexuality. One could no longer trust what people said about their motives, promises, or wishes. In fact, we didn't even know what our insides were telling us, and to the extent we did figure it out, we didn't like what we saw.

Whereas Freud generated an internal revolution—we could no longer trust our desires and our will to obey us (or even figure out *what* they were about)—Darwin worked on the "outside," the world or cosmos and our place in it. Our success at industrial, scientific, and colonization levels had led people to believe in human centrality and exceptionalism. We were vastly different from all other animals. Descartes claimed we were unique because we could "think"—the rational mind set us off absolutely from all other creatures, making us the only subjects, and everyone and everything else became mere objects. Hence it created a picture of human beings as rightful owners and users of the planet. *We* are living organisms, and everything else is more like a machine with removable parts that could be used without damaging the whole.

It is difficult for us to imagine how it felt to be the hegemonic human being in such a world. By "hegemonic," I mean the classic, desirable model of the human being: Western, young, male, white-skinned, well-to-do, educated, confident, Protestant, able-bodied. To be sure, most people did not fit this model: women, children, all non-Westerners, physically or mentally challenged, old, colored skin, poor, uneducated, and so on. Immanuel Kant said that one owed such people as himself—the hegemonic human being—moral regard; that is, one should treat such people fairly and justly. This human being is the "neighbor" that the New Testament says we should "love." The rest—all the other human beings, all other animals and life-forms of any sort, and certainly plants, trees, mountains, oceans, land, and so on—fell outside of "moral concern."

What is left, of course, is a small elite of the planet's inhabitants, less than 1 percent. So when Darwin claimed that we

came from and are similar to—let alone completely dependent on—all other life-forms, this elite club of human beings
felt threatened to the core. I recall my ancient New England
matriarchal aunt saying that certainly *she* was not related to
the apes! However, not only are we not at the top of the planet's
creatures, but we are the most vulnerable and least needed. If
we were to disappear tomorrow from the planet, everything
else would be better off. (Our pets would miss us for a few days
until they adjusted!)

Climate change is an excellent example of how far we
have fallen from our old status as the most powerful, bril-
liant, necessary animal on the planet to its worst enemy.
Climate change, which we now know is the result of our
greedy use of fossil fuels to energize our insatiable consumer
market economy—our triumph, as it were, over the planet's
resources—has boomeranged back on us as our greatest
threat. What we thought we could control, the planet's energy
to feed our insatiable desire for the comfort and pleasure of a
few (the 1 percent!), has come back to haunt us as the power
that may well be our death knell. What we thought was just
another "object" in our planet—the weather—has become
the greatest, most powerful "subject," whose agency we have
every right to fear as greater than ourselves. Can "weather"
act? Apparently yes, and act with awesome power. So far we
are defeated in our attempts to control or even to mitigate the
consequences of what we have let loose—the burning up of
our planet, our one and only home.

It is not only scary—it is terrifying. No wonder that most
teen literature these days is apocalyptic: young people's deepest fear is that they are losing their home (of course they cling
to their helicopter parents). But all of us deep down fear this.
It is the unacknowledged elephant in the room that many

of us avoid talking about. It is not discussed in polite society, the way sex and cancer were not discussed when I was a kid. *How* could we have come to this? We, the planet's darling and most complex, glorious creation—we can, after all, imagine the universe in our heads—have come to the point where we can also imagine our planet's demise, either quickly with a nuclear bomb or more slowly with climate change. We are at a fork in the road where we have never been before—capable of destroying our own home.

So we come to our third master of suspicion: Nietzsche and his notion of "ressentiment," a deep, pervasive fear that we are out of our depth, completely out of our depth. Nietzsche expressed it as "the death of God"—that is, the end of our confidence that regardless of our sins, we are in the hands of the Almighty God who would not let his children perish. We now need reasons to believe in our world, for without God, it is all up to us. Deep down, not only apocalyptic teenagers are afraid of the future, but we so-called grown-ups are also. We are *deathly* afraid. Without belief in God, however weak it is—just an assumption of our culture—even if *I* don't believe in God, others do. But if no one believes anymore, if even that cultural assumption is gone, then what stands in the way of a deep, pervasive, all-consuming despair? One might as well try to take care of one's tiny little corner of the world, since hope for the greater good, the "commons," is beyond us. This is not usually a "voiced" despair; rather, it is like a rotten stain throughout everything, a stain that cannot be erased. In fact, if asked to identify it, most of us could not. But we feel things are not right; there is something wrong at the core, but we do not know what. It used to be that "sin" was the problem, but "sin" meant something wrong with individuals, not with the whole world, as is now the case.

But now the stain has spread throughout the world, certainly the political but also the cosmic world. It is much bigger than any of us can handle. We are overwhelmed with its horrendous dimensions. The specters of climate change collapse and uncontrollable poverty as manifest in millions of immigrants are too terrifying to contemplate, especially if we—mere human beings minus a providential, caring, powerful God—have to deal with it. The economic world (market capitalism) and the biological (climate change) are both infected, and the issue seems totally beyond individual solutions, at the same time that our Western political systems are increasingly dysfunctional, especially the American system. "Things have gotten out of hand," and we despair of any solutions. Everything has gone awry, and a deep melancholy has settled over us. What should we do?

We are now ready, perhaps, to delve into some of the distinctive notes from postmodern thinking that I believe open up ways to help us see how a sacrificial life for others in our world, a world characterized by extreme inequality and climate change, might be relevant. We must give up the picture of ourselves as in control, as "managing" the planet, as deserving all the riches of the planet we can hoard for ourselves, as able to come up with the technological magic bullet for fighting climate change. What if we really opened our minds and hearts to a very different worldview that suggests a type of power that our society sees as wrong, ineffective, and maybe even foolish? What if we took the kenotic life and death of Jesus as our model and considered how contemporary science and postmodern reflection might help us live as Christians in our time?

One of the tasks that theologians have is to suggest to people alternative interpretations of the God/world relationship.

No one has ever seen God, so all talk about God is necessarily metaphorical—that is, assertions that say *something* about God but do not say all that needs to be said. As with all language about what we cannot see but is nonetheless important to us, such as love, peace, happiness, fear, death, and so on, we use what we *can* see to stand for what we cannot. Thus all religious and poetic language is metaphorical, and it is critical to use metaphors appropriate for our deepest experiences of these matters.

Thus I am suggesting that the phenomenon of climate change, which is destabilizing all our hopes and plans for human and planetary well-being, needs different metaphors from the standard monarchical one. It needs ones that are less individualistic and anthropocentric. It needs ones that are more social, relational, and immanent than the monarchical one.

The Story of Jesus

A powerful candidate is one that begins with the story of Jesus, particularly the story that underscores the self-sacrificial or kenotic character of all Jesus's words and actions. Such an interpretation is summed up in Philippians 2:5–8: "Let the same mind be in you that was in Christ Jesus, who, though he was in the form of God, did not regard equality with God as something to be exploited, but emptied himself, taking the form of a slave, being born in human likeness. And being found in human form, he humbled himself and became obedient to the point of death—even death on a cross." Here we see an inversion of the power in the monarchical model in preference for a kenotic, sacrificial model, "a joyous, kind and loving attitude that is willing to give up selfish desires and make sacrifices on behalf of others for the common good and the glory of God."[2] This is both a salvation and a discipleship model; that is, it speaks to how God "saves" the world, and it tells us human beings how we should act in the world. In this model, Jesus does not "do it all"—that is, suffer on the cross as a substitute for us, paying a price for our sins. Rather, it suggests that our salvation is patterned on Jesus's life and action: we join Jesus in living lives of sacrificial love for others and, as such, attain deification. We become like God. Made in the image of God, we become fully who we are, fully human, by participating in God's own life and love. Moreover, as some suggest (and I am among them), "kenosis is not only an explanation of Jesus' real humanity, but it is also the pattern of all reality."[3] The range of kenosis is understood here to be both broad and deep.

The Story of Evolution

For instance, we see our religious and secular lives coming together, for the same protoaltruistic actions that we see in evolution reach an epitome in the Christian understanding of the Trinity. Kenosis as "the pattern of all reality," from evolution to the Trinity, is a big assertion. How is this so? Holmes Rolston refutes Richard Dawkins's assertion of the survival of the "selfish gene," insisting instead that in evolution, "the survival of the fittest turns out to be the survival of the sharers." He asserts this position because in evolution, "fitness means dying to self for newness of life in a generation to come," thus suggesting an unconscious kenosis at the most basic biological level. Rolston writes, "The picture coming more and more into focus has a great deal of one kind of thing being sacrificed for the good of another. The lives of individuals are discharged into, flow into, 'emptied into' these larger currents of life."[4]

In fact, the process of evolution is nothing but this complex and continuous process of competition and interdependence. There is nothing mysterious about this process: all that is being claimed is that the upper levels of evolution depend on the lower levels in order for the complex, diverse world we actually have to exist. As Rolston says, "If the higher forms had to synthesize all the life materials from abiotic materials (also degrading their own wastes), they could never have advanced very far. The upper levels are freed for more advanced synthesis because they depend on syntheses (and decompositions) carried out by lesser organisms below."[5] And this process is precisely the one of death for the purpose of new (and more complex, diverse) life that we see everywhere about us. It is the process of life preying on life, since advanced life requires food pyramids, eating and being eaten. Thus while there is no kenosis in nature, there is limitation, struggle, sacrifice, and death everywhere: it is the heart of the process. Take Rolston's comment on plants, for example: "Seen in this more comprehensive scheme of things, plants function for the survival of myriads of others. We could say, provocatively, for our 'kenosis' inquiry, that they are 'emptied into,' given over to, 'devoted' to, or 'sacrificed' for these others in their community." But of course it is not just a one-way scheme. The plants also "benefit": "Plants become insects, which become chicks, which become foxes, which die to fertilize plants."[6] We must keep in mind, however, that none of this is conscious but is simply the way the system works. It works in a self-interested fashion but within a system of interdependencies that demands "sharing."

While it is not necessary for our purposes that we understand all the intricacies of the evolutionary process, it is essential that its major outlines, stressing both radical individuality and radical unity, be given full expression. Thus while "individualism" in the sense of existence by and for oneself is anathema in evolution, it is also the case that it works by "individuality"; that is, each part, no matter how small or large, makes its contribution to the creation of more and more complex and diverse forms of life. Hence were we to make a leap to the human scene, we could at least say that if reality is put together in this fashion, then it is impossible to imagine fulfillment for any individual apart from the whole. It is not as if individuality is added to the process when it reaches the human level; rather, we become the individuals we are only through the unimaginably old, complex, intricate, gradual process that has created all the individuals (of whatever species) in the world. At the very least, this new way of looking at individuality should make us open to contemplating the possibilities for the abundant life for human flourishing, not with terms such as *me* and *mine*, but with ones like *us* and *ours*.

Relational Ontology

What we see in evolution we see also in the story of Jesus and the Trinity: radical relationality. In contrast to Descartes's "I think; therefore I am," what we see emerging in evolution and in our interpretation of the Jesus story as well as its implications for understanding God is a different mantra, "I relate; therefore I am." What we see, in other words, is a "relational ontology" in which kenosis is a necessary first step at evolutionary, christological, Triune, and discipleship levels. Thus kenosis, the unconscious or conscious sacrifice of one for the other(s), shows that there is a correlation between the Trinity and the basic structures of the universe. The new story that we are suggesting is not merely a "religious" or a "secular" one but both, a story that stretches all the way from the most primitive one-celled creature to an understanding of God. However, while the sacrifice of one for the others is unconscious at the prehuman level, it must be conscious at our level—and this is very challenging. As John Zizioulas tells us,

> Communion with the other requires the experience of the *Cross*. Unless we sacrifice our own will and subject it to the will of the other, repeating in ourselves what our Lord did in Gethsemane in relation to the will of his Father, we cannot reflect properly in history the communion and otherness that we see in the triune God. Since the Son of God moved to meet the other, his creation, by emptying himself through the *kenosis* of the Incarnation, the "kenotic" way is the only one that befits the Christian in his or her communion with the other—be it God or one's "neighbour."[7]

In other words, there is no "escape" to "let Jesus do it," if we accept this story of relational ontology as basic to our universe.

The Stories Unpacked

From this sketch, we can see several features of this story. First, it must be anchored in an interpretation of the life and work of Jesus because Christians see God "in the face of Jesus." Second, it must be in line with the understanding of reality current in our time. In other words, one criterion is that the religious and the secular stories of our time must be compatible. Third, it must be an engaging, powerful story in order to replace the monarchical engaging powerful story. Do we have such a story? I believe we do, and I am trying to make a case for it.

First, the story of Jesus: There are many "stories" of Jesus, but here I will sketch just one as a substitute for the standard one. This story takes as its primary biblical text Philippians 2:5–8, where the central movement is the self-emptying of God, becoming incarnate in a humble human being whose eventual end is death on a cross. Unlike the standard model where God is expressed as a powerful overlord, here we have the complete reversal. According to Lucien Richard, "The self-emptying of Jesus is the revelation that to be God is to be unselfishness itself. Being God means to be the giver."[8] Whereas the monarchical model underscores God's power at all levels—in the creation as the Creator ex nihilo and on the cross as the One who heroically takes our sins upon himself— the kenotic story is completely different. It is a mystery how the two stories could exist side by side for hundreds of years when their foundations and implications are exact opposites. The kenotic Jesus, as the incarnate God, is epitomized in the Sermon on the Mount and in the parables in which reversals of the powerful and the powerless are common.

But the story of Jesus is *most* powerfully expressed in the cross. Jürgen Moltmann could not be more emphatic: "The death of Jesus on the cross is the *centre* of all Christian theology."[9] The standard interpretation of the cross claims it is central because here Jesus, as our substitute, relieves us of punishment for our sins. "Let Jesus do it all"—this mantra is the "faith" we need in order to be "saved," to inherit eternal life. A kenotic understanding of the cross is very different. To begin with, it tells us who God is. As Moltmann writes,

"When the crucified Jesus is called the 'image of the invisible God,' the meaning is that *this* is God, and God is like *this*. God is not greater than he is in this humiliation. God is not more glorious than he is in this self-surrender. God is not more powerful than he is in this helplessness. God is not more divine than he is in this humanity. The nucleus of everything that Christian theology says about 'God' is to be found in this Christ event. The Christ event on the cross is a God event."[10]

Because Christians see God in the life, teachings, and death of Jesus, kenosis, or self-sacrificing, is not just the story of Jesus, but it is also the story (interpretation) of God. Thus theology (theos-logos), "talk about God," begins with talk about Jesus. And it is talk about a kenotic Jesus, or as John Caputo puts it, "Suppose we think of God as someone who prowls the streets . . . disturbs the peace. . . . Suppose we imagine God as a street person with a definite body odor."[11] How shocking! The shock is necessary to save us from imagining Jesus and thus God in a sanitized, spiritualized way. The "incarnation" is a messy business, or it should be. It is about God as really, truly, deeply being one of us, one who is with us in all the dark, dreary, and shocking parts of our lives. As we have noted, Christians see God as both transcendent and immanent. However, Christians have emphasized, *overemphasized*, the transcendence of God. A kenotic theology demands that we start with and stay with immanence—that is, the worldly, fleshly, messy, despairing side of God. At the deepest level of "immanence," of God being present with us, are the calls to a form of self-sacrifice, calls very apt for our consumer culture: Jesus says in Matthew 19:21, "If you wish to be perfect, go, sell your possessions, and give . . . to the poor . . . then come, follow me"; in Luke 9:3, "Take nothing for your journey, no staff, nor bag, nor bread, nor money"; and in Matthew 16:24 KJV, "If any *man* will come after me, let him deny himself, and take up his cross, and follow me."

Kenosis as an Interpretation of Reality

These typical sayings by Jesus have always been hard for well-off people to brush aside. Surely, God does not expect *us* to follow him to this extent! However, if a kenotic theology includes discipleship, then we must admit that it does include our lives as well. Apparently, what is becoming clear is that a kenotic theology moves in several directions to include what we say about God and what we say about ourselves. In other words, it is a total interpretation, a new, different way of being in and understanding the world. It is saying that in order to get a glimpse of what this new worldview is about, begin with the lowly story of a carpenter who lived in a strange, self-sacrificial way—a way totally different from our selfish, consumer-oriented way—and yet a way where glimpses of both evolutionary and Trinitarian reflection were present. How odd that the countercultural life of an insignificant peasant should touch on such seemingly esoteric topics as evolution and the Trinity. What is going on here? It seems to be saying that kenosis is both a form of knowledge and a way to live. Is it suggesting that in clear opposition to individual human self-fulfillment (which is one interpretation of the twenty-first-century creed), a model of sacrificial love for the neighbor is not only "good" for the other but also close to "reality" as understood by evolutionary theory and some interpretations of the Christian understanding of God, the Trinity? Does all this loosely hold together—that is, give us a different picture of how to live on planet earth in the twenty-first century than the consumer, individualistic model?

Kenosis and the Great Exchange

This demanding discipleship is only possible because and as we participate in the life and love of God, in "the great exchange." Let us look more deeply into the kenotic track of interpretation. Michael Gorman summarizes it as "cruciform theosis."[12] What this phrase means is that divinity is qualified by the cross, that the cross takes place in, participates in, God. This kenotic track of interpretation suggests something entirely different from the standard Western story of Jesus, which, as we have seen, is a grim, negative one. The kenotic story suggests what the early church called "the great exchange." As Irenaeus puts it, "Our Lord Jesus Christ, who did, through His transcendent love, become what we are, that He might bring us to be even what He is Himself provided the most compelling and often-repeated form of the perennial *cur deus homo* for generations to come, even until today."[13] In other words, God (in Jesus Christ) became incarnate in humanity so that we, participating in Christ through the sacraments and our actions, might become God-like. The grand exchange is deep incarnation; it means that God is deeply, totally immanent in the flesh and, by implication, in all of creation—that the entire creation participates in, lives in, God. God lives in us, our world, and hence our world—and we humans by acknowledgment—live in God. This is an ontological statement about "reality." It is claiming that everything that is exists *because* it lives within God and therefore has a certain character—a "cruciform" character. Hence the signs of sharing, symbiosis, and life and death that we see in evolution and the pattern of give-and-take, of mutual reciprocity, in the Trinity are clues to the kenoticism inherent in the world. In other words, kenoticism, self-sacrificial behavior, is not strange but common; in fact, it is how the universe operates (says evolution), and it is how divinity operates (says the Trinity).

Hence the goal of kenotic interpretation is not negative but joyously positive, for it says this is the way both reality and God are. It does not say that everything will turn out as we wish or that death (and sickness, wars, etc.) will not take place, but it *does* claim that we live kenotically in God—not on our own but with God and with reality. Hence the grand exchange is indeed joyful, for through it, we participate in "the way things are," according to both reality and God. It claims that God participates in (is incarnate in) the world and the world exists within God: this is the way kenotic interpretation works. Thomas Merton expresses it in a personal, powerful, and persuasive way in the following passage: "Christ Himself . . . 'breathes' in . . . me divinely in giving me His Spirit. . . . The mystery of the Spirit is the mystery of selfless love. We receive Him in the 'inspiration' of secret love, and we give Him to others in the outgoing of our own charity. Our love in Christ is then a life both of receiving and of giving. We receive from God in the Spirit, and in the same Spirit we return our love to God through our brothers."[14] This wonderful passage expresses how the kenotic exchange works at the most basic, physical level—the level of each breath we take. With each incoming breath, we receive Christ's selfless love into ourselves, making it possible when we breathe out to do so selflessly. So Christ works *in* me, in my every breath (the ground of our physical existence), to make selfless love possible. Christ loves us selflessly with our intaking breath, empowering our physical being (our breath and our will) so that we can love selflessly.

A wonderful continuity is appearing here among various levels: personal, scientific, and religious. What Merton expresses at the level of the individual Christian trying to do the impossible—be a disciple of the kenotic, self-sacrificing Jesus—shows how this *is* possible. He is doing what religious folk have always done—use the deepest, most physical phenomenon of our lives (here the very breath that sustains us in life) as a metaphor for the greatest conundrum of the religious life in most traditions: how to love the neighbor. This seemingly simple universal law has proven to be impossible for human beings, even the most saintly ones.[15] But the grand exchange (God becoming incarnate in the world) means that with each breath we take, God is in us doing what we cannot—love the neighbor. Hence as we "exhale," we *can* love the neighbor, not with our own love, but with the only source of all life and love—God. Therefore, the "impossible" parables, the commands to "take up one's cross" and follow Jesus, are not impossible, not because we are acting, but because God is. God, who first reached out to us in the incarnation, has given us the power to love. What we see at a personal level of the lonely Christian trying to do the impossible—the saintly thing of loving the neighbor—is now empowered to do so. Such persons are channels of divine love, breathing *in* God's love to empower them and breathing God's love *out* in their actions.

What we see in the individual example we also see at scientific and religious levels. Thus the glimmers of kenosis, albeit unconscious, are seen in evolution in the pattern of death for the purpose of new life and all the different forms of it: symbiosis, sharing, interdependence, and so on. In other words, the world works this way—what empowers the incredibly diverse, complex, intricate give-and-take of evolution is in continuity with Merton's personal experience of how faith in Jesus works. And it is also in continuity with the

Christian Trinity: the movement of giving and receiving, the dance in which each "person" takes the lead and then passes it on, and on and on.

Kenosis and Discipleship

Certainly the way in which self-sacrificial love operates at these various levels is very different, yet the pattern is similar. It is not a movement in which one succeeds while all the others fail (the triumph of the individual); rather, it is a movement in which through sacrifice, new possibilities emerge. The "sacrifice" is not always fair, just, or pretty; in fact, it is often unfair and painful for some. It is neither a just nor a pretty story, but its believers claim it is the way the world works; hence it *must* be accepted. What religions such as Christianity claim is that the particular form of kenosis they practice is one that tries to take actions that help make up for the "losers" to the ones who suffer most.

Here we see another difference between the levels of kenosis: at the level where science functions, there are no operating agents who can attempt to make things more just. However, God's reaching out in the person of the Son (God incarnate in the world) offers the possibility of empowering love to even things out. So Christians do not claim that evolution is just; rather, what they suggest is that by God working through us, things *can* turn out differently. While no creature but us can choose to be a participant in the grand exchange, we can so choose to be empowered by love. In other words, the individual Christian (as well as religious bodies) looks for possibilities where sacrificial love can make a difference in worldly outcomes. Because we believe that God *is* kenotic love, self-sacrificial love, we have an ally in God for helping

21

the grand exchange take place even in the worst of worldly realities: Syria, the Holocaust, Rwanda, Hiroshima. The same power, sacrificial love that operates at the individual level, can also be active at public and scientific levels, helping the realities at these levels "bend" in the direction of kenotic love.

Are we assured of victory? Does God's will for sacrificial sharing always win? By no means. Ours is a "minimal" faith, operating with eyes wide open to the negativities of existence at both personal and other levels, refusing to turn from inconvenient truths, naming them as objectively as possible. And yet working with this faith, our hope remains open to the possibilities that God can bring about by working through us. We pray "to him who by the power at work within us is able to accomplish abundantly far more than all we can ask or imagine" (Eph 3:20).

ONE

The Kenotic Stories of Jesus and God

The Kenotic Story of Jesus

As we dig more deeply into kenoticism and its meaning both for Christianity and for climate change, we need to be reminded of an important qualification from Lucien Richard: "The only way in which a kenotic Christology can become intelligible is if it is perceived within the whole divine life and economy. A kenotic Christology must be rooted in the Trinitarian mystery; it must be evident in the creation and redemption of the world."[1] Elsewhere Richard adds, "Kenosis is a way of describing the divine being and the divine action in Jesus Christ. It describes not only who God is in Jesus Christ but also who the believer must be."[2] In other words, kenosis is a way of understanding Christian faith much like "individualism" has been for those Christians interpreting God as a superindividual, with human beings as lesser individuals.

But we human beings of the twenty-first century occupy an entirely different reality from that of our forebears. We live in a totally relational reality, where no individual exists by him- or herself; in fact, one of the best expressions of current understandings of reality is the Buddhist "dependent co-origination."[3] This notion suggests that each depends on all and all originate with all. It is difficult for most Westerners to envision, let alone embody, such a notion, given how thoroughly brainwashed we are by "individualism." And yet it is imperative that we begin to imagine "dependent co-origination," since it is far closer to reality as presently understood not only by various religions but also by the sciences. While dependent co-origination is commensurate with current evolutionary theory, it is also widespread in various religions, including some forms of Christianity. Kenoticism is one such form of Christianity. The kenotic story of Jesus is about God, as are all stories about Jesus. This is the case because Jesus is "the face of God" for Christians. Richard writes, "The true face of God is unveiled in the human face of Jesus."[4] It matters which story of Jesus we accept, since it determines to a large extent what we not only say about God but say surreptitiously. For we are seldom fully aware of the story that dictates our behavior; thus it is more powerful than we suspect.

In popular circles, the most widely accepted story of Jesus often passes as a "description" of the life and death of Jesus and hence will brook no opposition. The traditional story goes something like this: Jesus, the Son of God—and hence God's embassy—dies on a cross for the sins of all human beings, past, present, and future. Thus the all-powerful God's honor has been saved by his Son's substitutionary atonement, and we human beings are granted eternal life in heaven. There are several variations of this story, but its heart is the absolute honor and power of God upheld by the substitutionary atonement of the Son. Our only role is faith in Jesus as our savior.

The kenotic story of Jesus is significantly different at its center. One of the best early versions of this story is Philippians 2:5–11. It comes in Paul's interpretation of an early hymn, with the key passage as follows: "Let the same mind be in you that was in Christ Jesus, who, though [or because] he was in the form of God . . . emptied himself, taking the form of a slave. . . . And being found in human form, he humbled himself and became obedient to the point of death—even death on a cross."[5] The key difference between the traditional and kenotic stories of Jesus is the understanding of power. Rather than the linear, controlling view of power (which Jesus appeases with his death on a cross), the kenotic story has a counterintuitive view, which is expressed in weakness and vulnerability. Thus Jesus as the Son of God reveals God to be the One who empties himself of all common views of power in order to identify divinity with creation, especially the weakest, most oppressed parts of creation. Thus a new way to live (and die) is being introduced into the world, one in which self-emptying for the benefit of others (one's neighbors) is the new story.

There are several key points that we need to emphasize in this new story. First, the kenotic story of Jesus is the recovery of the relational self. Whereas the traditional story focuses on individual human beings benefiting from Jesus's substitutionary atonement on the cross, the emptying of the self in the new story is preparation for a new kind of life: a radically *relational* one where self-emptying is preparation for being filled with God and neighbor. By accepting a life of participation in God, one receives the power to love from God and passes it on to the needy neighbor. Above all else, the kenotic story of Jesus claims that the myth of individualism is a lie and that fulfilled human life must be relational. *There is no way to live as an isolated individual.* Contemporary evolution insists on radical interrelationship and interdependence, but so does kenotic Christian faith. Unless one is human as Jesus was human (as radical self-emptying for the neighbor), one cannot be human at all. Evolution and kenotic living both insist on radical relational existence.

The second implication of the new kenotic story insists on Jesus taking on the embodied, fleshly, earthly, human life. The incarnation, God taking on human flesh (another way to speak of God's self-emptying), means that fulfilled humanity has to do with bodily well-being. Hence healing and feeding bodies are central parts of Jesus's new kenotic story. The incarnation means that following Jesus is not principally a spiritual matter, but it has to do with the basics of life: food, water, health, education, and so on—whatever makes up the good, earthly life for various species.

The third significant difference between the two stories of Jesus is its "inclusion." As a story that insists upon the radical relationality of existence, its scope is wide—the kenotic story, similar to today's evolutionary story, insists that basic minimal life for each creature entails the inclusion of many different other creatures and earthly systems (such as weather, arable land, water, etc.). A story that focuses on the well-being of all creatures, who are interrelated and interdependent with many others, is an inclusive, mutually dependent interpretation of life that includes human beings but not as the sole actors in or as the only recipients of the story.

In fact, when one takes the three critical features of this Christian kenotic story together, what emerges is a story of empowerment of all through the dance of death and new life, sacrifice and renewal, mutual reciprocity. Jesus—in his life of countercultural compassion for the weak and forgotten elements of creation, including oppressed human beings, culminating in his sacrificial death—epitomizes kenoticism for Christians and is the finger pointing to the nature of God. Here we have a living, human expression of radical kenoticism for the "Other" that not only gives discipleship its paradigm but, as importantly, tells us of God.

After this analysis of the story of Jesus as the summary of kenosis, we see several issues that the story raises. First, it asks how widespread is kenoticism; second, it asks for a fuller picture of kenoticism in the New Testament; and third, it asks for a more complete picture of what this story tells us of God. We will supply a little filler for each of these concerns.

First, kenoticism is widespread in contemporary religions. In Buddhism, for instance, the notion of *sunyata* (emptiness) is similar to kenoticism. It stresses letting go of all attachments, and hence, presumably, it leaves the practitioner free of suffering. Moreover, the Buddhist notion of "dependent co-origination" is a powerful way to express the mutual dependence of all individuals on each other; in fact, dependent co-origination insists that there is no becoming alone. Individuals are the result of a fundamental activity of energy, so existents have no reality in themselves but are interdependent.

Moreover, the French philosopher Simone Weil's notion of "decreation" has similarities to both kenoticism and sunyata: "[Weil] practiced what she called 'decreation,' a form of self-emptying in which she sees herself diminish as God grows in her. Decreation, or the death of the will, is giving up control over one's life, so that God can subvert the self's exorbitant and constantly growing desires. The point is not mortification but a discipline of emptying herself so that God can be all in all."[6]

The unencumbered human individualism of Western theology now appears not only naïve but wrong. The world is much more complex and varied than we suspected, and science and religion appear much closer, since both now seem to rely on a combination of verifiable information *and* interpretation. Sacrifice and sharing, mutual reciprocity, death and new life, and giving and receiving are widespread in various religious cultures, including First Nations. They embrace stories of the lives of bears and salmon as comparable to human stories of loss and fulfillment. The pattern appears to be similar: the necessity of giving and receiving. Jesus did not invent the relation between the cross and new life but was only adding to a universal story of the way the world works: no new life except through death.

The second issue we will expand upon is a fuller picture of kenoticism in the New Testament and early Christianity by focusing on Irenaeus's contribution and on Paul's expression of kenoticism. The grand narrative that Irenaeus projects as deification, becoming like God (theosis), begins with the kenotic story of Jesus. Irenaeus adds an essential motif: the grand exchange in which God became human so that humans might become Godlike. This is unfortunately not a strong motif in Western theology, but we are the losers because of this oversight. The Eastern view of the grand exchange explains how salvation entails our participation in God's own life. This gift assumes from the very beginning that human beings are endowed with a closeness and likeness to God that potentially draw us *to* God. Thus the incarnation is not a "second thought" to repair the broken relationship between God and humans due to our sin, but it is what God planned from the beginning: that human beings (along with all other creatures) be invited *to live God's life*. This intimacy and joyous call to all *to participate in God's own life* is a long way from the negativity and coldness of the juridical story of Jesus repairing a ruptured relation between God and humans due to sin. For Irenaeus, the founder of the theosis doctrine, we were created with an affinity and likeness to God, which implies that the accurate story is one that has human beings longing for and being fulfilled by God.

The intimacy between God and human beings that Irenaeus supports is similar to the closeness of God and human beings in Paul. Thus, in a statement justly famous for its mystical intimacy, Paul says in Galatians 2:20, "It is no longer I who live, but it is Christ who lives in me. And the life I now live in the flesh I live by faith in the Son of God, who loved me and gave himself for me." This extraordinary passage where Paul seems to suggest that he is unclear who is acting—Christ or himself—is the new creation that follows Christ's death and resurrection. There are several important features to Paul's understanding of the master narrative that shape not only the story of Jesus but also all subsequent stories, such as yours and mine. First, it is not a mere imitation of Jesus but a transformation, a new birth, a new creation. Thus theosis (deification) for Paul involves not only cruciform living but also resurrected living. Paul does not focus on the cross alone, the place where Christ performs justification for our sins, for the negative justification is always seen together with the new resurrected life.

Second, for Paul, crucifixion is always cocrucifixion. That is, *we* are involved in our own salvation: what could be called "cruciform theosis."[7] Paul does not, as in much of Western theology, focus on substitutionary atonement for our sins but sees salvation in inclusive, joyous terms as the reenactment of the intimacy that God intended for all creation with the divine life. Thus the story of salvation is not limited to Jesus and the cross but has deep implications for disciples, for Paul sees himself and every believing individual and community as part of the narrative. According to Michael Gorman, *"For Paul, to be in Christ is to be a living exegesis of this narrative of Christ, a new performance of the original drama of exaltation following humiliation, of humiliation as the voluntary renunciation of rights and selfish gain in order to serve and obey."*[8] Thus the Pauline view of the new Christian life is a complete one with notes of both the cross (kenotic sharing in the burdens and unfair oppressions of earthly life) *and* the joyous, resurrected life, which is already partially present. Hence if "cruciform theosis" is the form of the new life in Christ, it will have motifs of not only cruciform (mutual sharing of earthly resources for the well-being of all created life-forms) but also joy (moments of inclusive peace and harmony, glimmers of the resurrected life to come).

The final (as well as the source) of Paul's understanding of the God/world narrative is the Trinity. One could say that the story begins and ends with the Trinity, for it provides the best expression of the nature of God and the accompanying nature of creation. The central feature of the kenotic story of Jesus is its witness to and expression of the nature of God, the Trinity. The Trinity is the heart, the essence, of God, of who God is in God's self. But an important caveat now appears: the kenotic story of Jesus does not point to the Western Augustinian model of the Trinity, which, based on aspects of a human individual, supports a substantial, static view of the Trinity as similar to a human individual. This emphasis underlies Western Christian theology supporting a view of God as a supernatural individual. The Eastern Orthodox view of the Trinity, on the other hand, stresses the three "persons" in constant, reciprocal, loving activity, thus promoting the picture of the Trinity not as a superhuman being but as universal, loving *activity* constantly expressing itself in creation as empowering, inclusive self-emptying love for others.[9] While I will use the handy tags of "Western" and "Eastern" views of the Trinity, I should mention two qualifications. First, the two views are not historically as sharply delineated as I have suggested, but for the sake of clarity, I have emphasized the differences. Second, while I am identifying the "individualistic" view with the Western church and the "kenotic" with the Eastern, that is only partially true, since the positions are historically much more diverse than I suggest. However, the individualistic view has influenced Western culture very deeply. The two types I call "Western" and "Eastern" are partly historically based and partly ideal types.

Nonetheless, the difference between these two stories is critical because the first one expresses a view of God as a supernatural, static being who is not credible in view of twenty-first-century science, whereas the other view of the Trinity is consonant with evolutionary and quantum science, stressing constant change, energy, and reciprocal mutuality. Christianity should be an affront to greedy, consumer-oriented visions of creaturely life, but it should *not* be an affront to the intellect. That is, theologians have the duty to interpret Christian faith as consonant with the science of the day so that disciples are not forced to dualistic interpretations—one religious and one secular. Rather, the disciples ought to be able to live a holistic, integrated life of the mind, although aware at the level of the will, this often countercultural faith will be opposed to the greedy consumer story in one's society.

In summary, the central reason the story of Jesus we choose to believe (and to follow in our lives) is important is that *it tells us about God*. While the traditional story is outmoded, is unbelievable to most, and contains a hurtful view of one-way, imperialistic power, our kenotic story tells us that the heart of God is self-emptying compassion for all of creation. It is a joyous story of divine limitation giving freedom to creation and divine love bent on maximal flourishing of all creation. Not only does the traditional story focus on a negative aspect of divine-human relations—that is, human sin demanding divine forgiveness—but it lacks much of a positive dimension. The kenotic story, on the other hand, while seemingly negative in its insistence on self-emptying, is actually positive because of its understanding of self-emptying. One New Testament critic says this of Philippians 2:5–11: "If the hymn exposes one paradox in its proto-Christology, it is that no exaltation is possible without humbling; no fulfillment is possible without emptying."[10] Another critic frames Jesus's words in Mark 8:35 with a similar remark: "Jesus in his own life and death, has universalized a fundamental law: 'whoever would save his life will lose it and whoever loses his life for my sake and the gospel's will save it.'"[11]

The Kenotic Story of God

We recall the central motif of the kenotic story of God by this statement from Richard: "The true face of God is unveiled in the human face of Jesus."[12] The reason we emphasize this is because the kenotic story of God starts at a different place than does the traditional story: the traditional story begins with God, while the kenotic story begins with Jesus. This is important because the story of Jesus in the New Testament is our main source for information about God. We have never seen God—no one ever has—so how can we begin to talk about

God? The answer is with the modest hints we have in the New Testament, which provide us with the main outlines of a doctrine of God. In fact, the kenotic story of Jesus gives us our supreme claim: "Kenosis is not a self-emptying in the form of a renunciation of the nature of God himself, but a self-emptying that is the very nature of God himself."[13] This amazing statement expresses the astonishment that we humans often feel to learn that "self-emptying" (kenosis, or cruciform compassion) is the very nature of God.

As we learn from Philippians 2:5–11, "This creative God is revealed most expressly in the incarnation: the God who reveals God's self in love to an Other and who, thus, becomes vulnerable to all the world's pain, injustice, suffering, and tragedy."[14] What wonderful news this is! It means that God is not some absolute, abstract, all-powerful deity whom we must fear; rather, the center of all of God's activities is a most extraordinary, self-emptying, compassionate love for the world and everything in it. It is God's nature "to go the second mile," "the tenth mile," "the umpteenth mile" for the creation, a nature most adequately expressed by the cross itself, its stunning inversion of power that undercuts every controlling expression and claims that real "power" is self-emptying love. How can that be? Kenosis is an entirely different description of what empowers the world than the traditional story's linear, imperial understanding of power. What *really* empowers both God and reality is self-sacrificial giving (one's life) in order that new life might appear. Thus evolution is one version of this dynamic, but so is God's life, for both function by giving and receiving, death and new life, interrelationship and interdependence. Evolution expresses altruism in a minimal fashion, while the kenotic story of God expresses maximal altruism. Thus kenosis addresses the nature of reality—of what makes the world "tick," as it were. And here the kenotic story insists that "reality" is empowered by a strange counter-cultural form of sacrificial action, which we see exemplified in Jesus's story and implicit in evolution throughout the rest of creation. This is very surprising—and joyous—news.

We need now to consider several questions about the heart of the kenotic story of God, the Trinity. We recall the difference between the Western (substance priority) and Eastern (relationality priority) versions of the Trinity. As Wesley Wildman summarizes the difference, "The basic contention of relational ontology is simply that the relations between entities are ontologically more fundamental than the entities themselves. This contrasts with substantivist ontology in which entities are ontologically primary and relations ontologically derivative."[15] The Western view of the Trinity has contributed to substantive thinking (a supernatural God), while the Eastern view has emphasized relational ontology (a kenotic God). The distinctive mark of the Western version is its individualism.

However, the Trinity is perhaps the most off-putting of any Christian doctrine. It is widely ridiculed as a puzzle: How can one be three or vice versa? Is the Trinity meant to be a mystery that is best left alone? If so, why are we bothering to try to understand it? Does Christianity really need the Trinity? Have we not just affirmed the statement that the cross is the center of Christian theology? So why concern ourselves with such a confusing, abstract problem as the Trinity?

The answer is *because nothing is more important*. The story of Jesus is significant as "a finger pointing to the moon," as to what it tells us about God. We have already hinted at two interpretations of the Trinity: one identified with the West (and Augustine) and the other with the East (and the Orthodox

Church). A sketch of the Western interpretation of the Trinity will answer some of our questions and issues. The distinctive mark of the Western version is its *individualism*. Augustine's metaphor of choice for the Trinity was a single individual with three functions or modes of being: Father, Son, and Holy Spirit. The following quotation from John Zizioulas, an Orthodox theologian, describes the impact on Western anthropology and worldview of this view of the Trinity: "Our Western philosophy and culture have formed a concept of man out of a combination of two basic components: *rational individuality* on the one hand and *psychological experience and consciousness* on the other. It was on the basis of this combination that Western thought arrived at the conception of the person as an *individual* and/or a *personality* that is a unit endowed with intellectual, psychological and moral qualities centered on the axis of consciousness."[16]

We in the West find such an interpretation commensurate with the common thinking of our culture. The central motifs of this interpretation of the human being paint a picture of a rational individual, psychologically oriented with a bent toward inward focus and a premium on individual achievement. We meet this individual in our Western novels, built as they are on individuals (usually male) in search of their identities. The current social media is a cornucopia of individualistic narcissism (with its flood of personal blogs and memoirs). The distinctive characteristic of this picture is its obsession with individual achievement at all costs. It lies at the base of the so-called American dream: individuals attempting to find their fulfillment on their own, regardless of the consequences to other human beings and/or the rest of nature.

Thus in this view, the Trinity becomes a superindividual, glorious in its isolation and superiority but scarcely credible within twenty-first-century contemporary science. Where does this God abide? How can such a supernatural being relate to lowly, natural creatures? What is the outlook or "bias" of this great being in the sky? Why should we care about such a God? While few might consciously care about this Trinitarian God, the subconscious influence of its story is immense, as we have seen. It invades our dreams, our desires, and our goals to a shocking degree, which we consider "normal" and desirable.

In fact, "individualism" often passes as a description rather than an interpretation. However, "passing as a description" is a victory, since we live in it as the "truth." In other words, the reason individualism has invaded our personal and public lives so thoroughly is that to most Westerners, it seems normal, natural, "the truth." Thus we see how important "language" is. For human beings, words are not "just words"; rather, they are our world. We construct the world (worldview) we live in, and this "world" in turn constructs us. The constant, subversive role of words thus becomes evident to us. Hence *it is critical which words we use to live by*. Words matter because human beings, unlike any other animal, construct (in part) the worlds in which we live. We participate in "the social construction of reality." The reason this is such a critical bit of awakening is that unless it occurs, people believe their opinions, interpretations, and biases *are* the truth. It then becomes impossible to see other points of view and thus to compromise with other opinions.

Moreover, this individualistic picture also eliminates the rest of the cosmos from consideration. As Zizioulas puts it, succinctly, "One has simply to look at the predominant forms of Christian worship and spirituality or at the prevailing theories of the atonement and the sacraments: in all cases the cosmic dimension of man is missing; man in his relation to God singles himself out from nature as the autonomous self, as if his capacities and incapacities had nothing to do with those of the entire cosmos."[17] The phenomenon of Donald Trump powerfully illustrates what extreme individualism (narcissism) can look like when invading every aspect of life. The West has seldom had such an excellent example of individualism "gone awry." No individual can exist alone: this is what contemporary science tells us, but the American story, at both personal and public levels (capitalism), tries to do so. This view of things has been tried, and it has failed, as the American experience of Trump illustrates to a shocking degree. However, the kenotic story of Jesus as "the face of God" implies not only a critique of individualism but also a very different view of God and of human life.

As we turn to the Orthodox Church to learn more about this other view, we see immediately that here the kenotic story focuses on the Trinity. Vladimir Lossky puts it strongly: "The Trinity is for the Orthodox church the unshakable foundation of all religious thought, of all piety, of all spiritual life, of all experience."[18] Hence it is difficult to imagine what does *not* fit under and within the Trinity! However, the Eastern view begins with the "three" as persons, not with the "one" as an individual. We have seen the results of the Western model of the Trinity, beginning with a single individual: it produces a view of God as "monotheistic substance," a static, unrelated superbeing. By focusing on the three persons in reciprocal relations of loving self-sacrificial activity, the Eastern Trinity is radically different. The Eastern view is not of *any* being but of *radical relationality*. By starting with "persons," the East lifts up relationship as central. Whereas an "individual" may be complete in him- or herself, persons, whether divine or human, are defined through *relations with others*. Thus, as Kallistos Ware writes, "God is a triunity of persons, loving each other, and in their reciprocal love the three persons are totally one without losing their specific individuality."[19] Likewise, Zizioulas says, "the human being is *defined* through otherness. It is a being whose identity emerges only in relation to other beings, God, the animals and the rest of creation. It is almost impossible to define the human being substantially."[20] This point is so critical that we need to underscore it: by the East turning to the constant activity of loving relations (the Trinity) as its metaphor, it understands both God and human beings as defined by otherness, by their relations, not by substances called "human being" or "God." In other words, we should consider relationality to be more basic than "being" because it is radical relationality that forms beings, whether divine or human.

The second major difference between Western and Eastern theologies is their views of salvation: the focus on individuality or relationality. The West is concerned mainly with the redemption of one individual, the human one, whereas the East cares about the well-being—in fact, the "deification"—of the whole created order. Thus while human individuals need divine intervention to atone for their sins, the Eastern concern focuses on the participation of the entire cosmos in God's life. This Western view is not only narrowly directed to the human being, but it is also negative, concerned mainly with eliminating human sin. The Eastern view, on the other hand, is inclusive, incarnational, and hopeful, focusing not only on the whole creation but on God's sharing his own life with creation. This interpretation supports a radical and deep incarnation: God's embodiment is not only in the brief human life of Jesus but also in the potential deification of the entire creation. Thus the self-emptying (kenosis) of the divine can be seen in the Trinity as one "person" passes life along to the next "person" and in the cross as it expresses the same pattern of death and new life. In both the Trinity and the cross, one sees the movement of kenosis to theosis (from self-emptying love as the mark of true love, whether divine or human, to deification of the entire created order). In summary, while in the West, the goal of theology is redemption from sins for individuals, in the East, the goal is an invitation to the entire creation to live by participating in God's own life.

We are beginning to see and hopefully appreciate the differences between two Christian interpretations of the nature of God and our own nature. Whereas in the West, the Trinity is often either an embarrassment or not understood (and hence plays a minor role in many Western theologies), in the East, the Trinity is *all*. Zizioulas puts it bluntly: "It would be unthinkable to speak of the 'one God,' before speaking of the God who is 'communion,' that is, of the Holy Trinity." Elsewhere, he puts it even more strongly: "Outside the Trinity there is no God." Thus translated, this means "*to be* and *to be in relation* becomes identical." In other words, the lonely human individual is not possible, because as we learn from the Trinity, relationship is primary. Again, Zizioulas says it well: "The expression 'God is love,' (1 John 4:16) signifies that God 'subsists' as Trinity, that is, as person and not as substance." And finally, Zizioulas sums up why this is important: "Thus love ceases to be a qualifying—i.e. secondary—property of being and becomes *the supreme ontological predicate*."[21]

It is difficult to overstate the difference this makes: it means that love is God's "name"; God is not "a being" of any sort but *love itself*. And it means further that God (as the Trinity) defines love, as known by us through the kenotic (self-sacrificing) activity of Jesus. Mark A. McIntosh expresses the importance of this interpretation: "God's hiddenness has to do with the heart-stopping, breath-taking freedom of the three divine Persons to give themselves away in love to each other and so to us and all creation—it is this which is truly incomprehensible."[22] It is critical that we absorb what this means: the entire cosmos is governed not by a neutral (and certainly not a malevolent) being but, on the contrary, by the constant activity of love both in itself and throughout creation. To be a Christian means to participate in God's own life, which is one of eternal self-sacrificing love. This means above all that the "heart" of the cosmos is self-giving love. What an amazing thing to say—and to believe! Our deepest fear that "reality" is neutral or malevolent is answered by *love* as God's name.

We come, then, to a final set of consequences from attending to the Trinity as the pattern for the nature both of God and of ourselves: discipleship. Ware states it well: "As an icon of the Trinity, I become truly myself only if I face others, looking into their eyes and allowing them to look into mine."[23] Indeed, looking into another's eyes is a powerful experience, a haunting experience, of how we are constituted: "I need you in order to be myself." When we have done this with another animal, preferably a nonhuman one for maximum effect, we have acknowledged that our selfhood is social: a human being is not egocentric but exocentric. We become human not by retreating to our inner being but by facing outward, toward the world—and others. As we consider what kenotic self-emptying means for us human beings, again we marvel at the differences between the Western and Eastern views. Here there is no retreat to the inner self. On the contrary, as McIntosh states, *"I am never more myself than when I give myself away for my neighbor in love."*[24] This one sentence can stand as the only thing we need to pay attention to. It raises neighbor love to central status for knowing both who we are and what we should do. In the simple command "to love the neighbor," one can see the divine plan: "the will and plan of God in everything—a will characterized by the divine delight in the other and measureless self-sharing."[25] Or as another commentator sums it up, "God disclosed as 'persons in communion' reveals a totally shared personal life at the heart of the universe."[26]

On the one hand, we rejoice in and can scarcely believe that love is at the heart of the universe and that God delights in limitless self-sharing. As well, the command to human beings to love the neighbor sounds relatively simple and straightforward. However, when we probe more deeply into what it means—that the basic principle of Christian faith is *the displacement of the self* in response to the self-emptying of God—we realize how challenging it is. We hesitate at the words "displacement of the self," for if one understands sin as a focus on one's own ego (or self), then we realize that the retreat of the self is the hardest thing a human can attempt. "Possession" is sin; "giving the self away" is righteousness. What is being asked of us is at the center of our identity. Is human identity reached through solitary, inner development (as the West often claims), or is it the opposite: *giving the self away for the Other*?

If the latter, then what assurances do we have that we will not be deserted in our self-emptying action? And here at this point is a clue: in our action of self-emptying for the neighbor, the removal of our own ego's "protection," we practice having faith that *God's own life will fill the void*. Self-emptying is practiced so that we can respond positively to God's invitation to *participate in the divine life*. If God is not a being but the perfection of love for the Other, then we do not have to love the neighbor on our own, so to speak. Rather, God loves the neighbor, loves all others, and we humans are invited to join the cosmic dance of receiving and giving that is, at the same time, the action of the Trinity—and, at another level, also the action of evolution. Hence we see a hidden truth emerging here in both the Trinity and biological evolution— a pattern of death and new life, of self-sacrificial love that results in new forms of life. We are called to give up our little egos in order to join the divine cosmic dance of sacrifice and new life.

It is not necessary that Christians know all the fine points of evolution or the intricacies of Trinitarian interpretation. In fact, excessive focus on either of these scholarly enterprises might obscure the main point that informed laypeople need to know. And this main point is critical: *we cannot live alone*. In fact, both religion (Christianity) and science tell us the same thing: "individualism" is a false story, whereas *radical interrelationship* is at the heart of both science and most religious stories. We come finally to summarize the two ways to interpret the Trinity, ways we have called Western and Eastern. Each of these Trinitarian interpretations derives from different stories of Jesus. In the Western version, the story is of an individual who died for the sins of all humankind and who points to a God who, as all-powerful, presumably could control climate change. The Eastern story of Jesus is of a "finger pointing to the moon." The story of Jesus's self-sacrificial love in his teachings and death points to the Trinity, that cosmic dance of sacrifice, sharing, and mutual interdependence. If the "God" of this tradition were to participate in climate change, it would be as the love that moves the stars calling to human beings to participate in God's plan of flourishing for all life-forms. Thus no static, deistic God pulls some ropes to magically save human beings from the consequences of climate change. Rather, we are being invited—no, *called*—to join the power of love in the universe in fulfilling God's intention that *all* may flourish.

TWO

Postmodern Insights for Climate Change

With the new worldview coming to us from various corners of postmodernism, we have a rich set of insights to join company with the kenotic view of Christianity in our attempt to provide an answer to the turning point of climate change. The contributions from postmodernism are deep and broad, ranging from changing our place from "outside" nature to "inside," with the accompanying change in both epistemology (how we know) and ontology (who we are). This is a profound shift that affects both our basic worldview and our behavior. We will look at Timothy Morton's "ecological thought" and Karen Barad's "agential realism" to see how postmodernism has changed "who we are in the world" and "how we know the world." We will then summarize some of the postmodern insights relevant to our project of a kenotic theology and climate change.

"Who We Are in the World" (Timothy Morton) and "How We Know the World" (Karen Barad)

With Timothy Morton's "ecological thought," we human beings move from our imagined standpoint as "outside" nature, and thus as "transcendent" over the world, to our more honest place as entirely "inside" nature.[1] Thus "nature" as a reality external to us disappears. It is an illusion, a dangerous one, about our place in the scheme of things. To the extent we live within this lie, we are unable to live fruitful lives on our planet because we believe ourselves to be in charge of the world and able to manage it. Capitalism is an example of our wrong-headed, false, and dangerous thinking. It has resulted in vast human financial inequality and a deteriorating planet.

The "ecological thought," on the other hand, is the admission of our total connection within our planet, so completely inside that we are like fish trying to explain what water is. Buddhists use the expression "dependent co-arising" to suggest how everything emerges through coexistence—nothing "exists" by itself. Hence in evolution, life-forms do not "adapt" to their environment but evolve along with it. We are, at this time in evolutionary history, the most complex, nuanced product of the planet's fifteen-billion-year-old history of evolution from a tiny bit of matter to all the complex, varied, wonderful life-forms on earth. Each and every part of us, from the bacteria in our gut to our opposable thumb and our magnificent brain, is a product of millions of years of tiny mutations in that initial bit of matter. As the most complex example of evolution, we are more "inside" the planet than anything else. We, who think we rule over and are superior to our planet, are actually its most amazing product—and a very vulnerable one. Our evolution is so amazing that we have ended up being able to imagine our creator (the planet) as *our* creation: we can hold a picture of the planet in our minds and imagine that it lies within our power to control. It is as if a child believed that it was/is its own parent. The story of our emergence from a spoonful of matter to our present reality is so slow, complex, mysterious, and amazing that we have trouble believing it. Take but one feature: our thumb. Tracing that one distinctive human characteristic throughout the billions of years is beyond human capacity. Yet it is the task we should undertake if we are ever to truly imagine our incarnation, our embodiment, from *within* the planet.

The heart of evolution, then, claims to be a continuous story with no dualisms and plenty of fuzzy edges between connections, which is radically different from our standard interpretation. Consider just one example—sex and sexual orientation. Rather than strict divisions between male and female, heterosexual and homosexual, and so on, evolution says that we are all male and female, straight and gay, in different ways and to different degrees. Likewise, features that we used to imagine were uniquely human—such as thinking, grieving, playing, sympathizing, and so on—are being discovered in other animals. Our exceptionalism and the radical dualistic divisions among life-forms are being questioned. Hence Martin Buber's addressing a tree as "thou" or a child playing that she is a tiger is not pure fantasy or merely primitive behavior. The false picture of ourselves culminated with the Enlightenment interpretation of the *human individual* as the epitome of evolutionary success. This picture is the total opposite of our true status, being made clear to us now in the disaster of climate change. Our helplessness before this twenty-first-century phenomenon is forcing us to acknowledge our false self-image. We have taken a selfie of ourselves posed on top of planet earth, but with our feet teetering on the edge as we try to save ourselves from plunging to our death.

So it is understandable why it is difficult for us to accept "the ecological thought" when we have lived for several centuries in the lie that this planet is ours for the taking, providing us with endless food and shelter. We are now being told that even our best environmental interpretations, ones where other life-forms are not simply oriented toward our well-being, are inadequate. Actually, the postmoderns say that we live with other creatures not as a community but as an origami, or a mesh network, or a rhizome set of roots and sprouts. The models we should now follow are not hierarchical but horizontal, not of a kingdom but of a democracy and even a biocracy, including all creatures, especially sentient ones, within the circle of our moral concern.

However, "the ecological thought" is not that of a cozy, harmonious kind of relationship. It is not on the model of an organism where every part has its place and contributes to the overall well-being of the whole. Rather, it is "connectionism" through differences, the microscopic mutations in the evolutionary story that connect us all through a complex mix of law and chance. The kinds of connections we see in evolution—composed of billions, zillions, of mutations in ways beyond our ability to imagine—connect us to other beings and other things. Such interdependence goes all the way down to every cell in our bodies; how each of us is "created" within the fifteen billion years of the earth's history is a process that has no center, no design, no goal. In addition, the more one knows about "the ecological thought," the more one realizes that *everything* is included, even our own shit, and as a matter of fact, in a highly populated consumer-capitalist society, we are surrounded by our own waste to a terrifying extent.

As Morton insists, consciousness "sucks," and as T. S. Eliot insisted, human beings cannot bear very much reality. "The ecological thought," then, is not only the pleasant rolling hills of English romantic poetry; it is also the piles of garbage produced by every major city.

The implications of moving in this direction are, of course, immense—from what and how we eat to land claims, education content and styles, financial justice, and so on. Would not every aspect of human dwelling on our planet change at a deep level if we were to see ourselves not as the owners of our planet but as one of its most needy occupants? Would it not also change our understanding of the divine, of what is sacred, from a blown-up version of a superman to—well, what and who? Morton suggests that at the very least, it should cause us to move away from our macho Western sky god to a more receptive, open, compassionate, sacrificial picture of the divine. If we believe that the model of ourselves and the model of God are interrelated—we are made in the image of God and God is understood on the model of ourselves—then these two issues will always be considered together. Therefore, how we imagine God and how we imagine ourselves are dangerous issues and should be handled with care. Would we not, at least, see ourselves as within God, as living and moving and having our being within God (with the world understood, perhaps, as God's body), rather than of God as a supernatural, distant, isolated being controlling but not being influenced by the world? Our goal is to try to reimagine who we are in the world, and I suggest here is a good start: we live within our world and within God.

We have been looking at ourselves "within nature," but Karen Barad's agential realism is an attempt to retain some measure of objectivity against extreme positions of knowing, doing, and being. Barad rejects both naïve realism and social constructivism. A one-paragraph summary of her somewhat daunting thesis is as follows: "In summary, the universe is agential intra-activity in its becoming. The primary ontological units are not 'things' but phenomena—dynamic topological reconfiguring/entanglements/relationalities/(re)-articulations. And the primary semantic units are not 'words' but material-discursive practices through which boundaries are constituted. This dynamism *is* agency. Agency is not an attribute but the ongoing configurations of the world."[2] Hers is a vision of reality that denies the radical separation of subject and object as well as other forms of dualism. Her phrase "exteriority within" attempts to summarize her position, which rejects the Cartesian model of "outside/inside" (subject vs. object, humans vs. the world), substituting for it a model where everything is "inside" but that saves a measure of "objectivity." She is against dualism and stasis, opting for a form of "differentiation in motion." She asks, How can we have an immanental picture of reality and still retain a place for both change and responsibility? Agential realism says that agents of all kinds (human and nonhuman, living and dead) construct the world but are not totally absorbed by it. In fact, the kind of immanentalism she imagines depends on difference (diffraction) rather than on sameness (reflection). The entire "mechanism" by which her picture of reality operates is by difference—nothing would "happen" without differences. However, while neither humans nor any other subject totally constructs or controls reality, humans are not entirely determined by it. We have agency (and hence responsibility) in and for the world.

The critical thing is trying to imagine ourselves as "inside" the reality that we help construct but of which we are also a product. We are both player and product of reality. The world is an "inside" job—an immanental picture that is constantly changing—of which we are a major player but certainly not the only one and increasingly a vulnerable one. It is probably impossible to describe Barad's interpretation of reality, since we are so thoroughly embedded in it. One analogy, however, that comes to mind is panentheism as a model of the God/world relation. In that model, the world and human beings are imagined as within God who embraces the world but is not identical with it or reduced to it. God and the world are intrinsically entangled with one another, but God and the world are also separate. In relation to God, the world (especially we human beings) is never apart from, standing outside of, or able to "describe" God. Likewise, the first step in understanding agential realism is to change where we are "standing," the point of view from and in which we imagine both our construction of and our dependence on the world. Barad is telling us to move from the privileged (but false) position of standing outside the world and talking about it—what it is, who is responsible for it, and so on—and deal with the very different picture of ourselves and our world when we put ourselves totally within reality. The only difference between us and other major subject players in the world is that we have self-consciousness—we know that we know. And what we know must start with the recognition that while our point of view gives us the rare privilege of knowing about the world (both its glories and its horrors), it does not change our place in the world, which is inside, like everything and everyone else.

The point is to overcome our allegiance to a subject/object epistemology and ontology in regard to our understanding of reality. We aim to move from a static, essentialist,

substance view to one that pictures reality as always changing and in which its quasi subjects and objects (what Barad
calls "phenomena") are made and unmade. The players in
this view of reality are not only human beings (and not even
just "the living") but everything that makes a difference. This
means that agency is wide open: What is there that does not
make a difference? Hence one is always dealing with continuity (subjects, objects, etc. compose the world but always
in different ways and to different degrees). This revised picture sees everything as *becoming*. Agency need not be human
or conscious, for agency covers whatever matters, whatever
makes a difference. So while there are not solid subjects in
this way of thinking, there are phenomena that in different
ways and to different degrees participate in the building of
the world. All are subjects and all are objects; hence *agential
realism* is an appropriate term for different kinds of agency
creating reality, creating the world.

If we accept our inside place, we make a huge jump that
will influence everything else we say about selves, other forms
of life, other bits of matter, and so on. Where we stand—on a
hillside on top of and outside the rest of the world or within
the world in the most radically entangled, embedded fashion imaginable—is the first change we must make. Then, but
only then, can we look for quasi descriptions, analogies, pictures, and so on that will help us say more about the world
and who we are in it—and in it in some interesting, distinctive ways. We are agents, subjects, but so are some unlikely
candidates, such as "climate change," that may not know
they are players but surely are. Our epistemological advan-
tage is a plus and a minus: it allows us to shout with joy on
a gorgeous Vancouver spring morning when the cherry trees
are blooming; however, it also makes us aware that not only

will this beauty end but so will we. Living with the joy and the terror of existence is the distinctive human experience.

Conclusion

As a summary model of the postmodern view, I would suggest Gilles Deleuze's picture of an origami. Here the same material is used over and over again, designed into billions of different forms of matter. In this model, we see the world and all of its folding and unfolding, with the same material recycled into different shapes and modes of complexity. Our worldview is not one of hierarchy, substance, dualism, or subjects and objects but one of a continuous borrowing and sharing, inter-dependence, death and new life. We need to begin to think about ourselves not as the masters or even the highest beings on our planet but as part of a biocracy, which includes all creatures, who, therefore, as in a democracy, have intrinsic value and "rights." Again, the one thing that distinguishes us apart from our particular form of rationality is our awareness of responsibility. We have become the one creature who knows that we live within the billion folds that make up our "origami" planet. We do not own or control it, but we can influence how it folds and who is included within the folds—at least to some degree.

Another attempt at a summary is Jane Bennett's riff on the Nicene Creed: "I believe in one matter-energy, the maker of things seen and unseen. I believe that this pluriverse is traversed by heterogeneities that are continually *doing things*. I believe it is wrong to deny vitality to nonhuman bodies, forces, and forms, and that a careful course of anthropomorphization can believe that encounters with lively matter can chasten my fantasies of human mastery, highlight the common materiality of all that is, expose a wider distribution of agency, and reshape the self and its interests."[3]

Finally, a summary of postmodernism from a more homely standpoint of a human being: How does it feel to be a human being living on planet earth in the twenty-first century with eyes wide open? It feels like radical relationality at all levels and ways—relationality is the primary feature of postmodernism. Moreover, it is a relationality from the "inside" as we humans participate in what we know: we are thoroughly embedded in the earth in both our knowing and our doing. We are not primarily "individuals" but exist only in community and within interrelatedness at cosmic, microscopic, and quantum levels. We often have a sense of wonder and awe the more we engage "eye to eye" with other species and realize how complex, diverse, and rich the world is. While we are increasingly aware of our vulnerability (and even disposability) on planet earth, nonetheless, we also feel increasingly responsible for the state of the planet, as our awareness of climate change grows. We are no longer the primary species on the planet, with all others inferior to us as mere "objects." More than anything else, we humans see ourselves as thoroughly embedded in our world, with one distinction—we are self-conscious. We know that we know, and what we know is that we are totally the product of evolution—and yet of an evolutionary pattern that functions on a pattern of new life through death. Some religions, including Christianity, take this model of self-sacrifice as the way to planetary flourishing and personal fulfillment.

THREE

Divine and Human Relational Ontology

Having accepted the shift from "outside" to "inside," we must turn to what difference it makes to be "inside" in terms of the postmodern view of transcendence and immanence. It is the movement from the supernaturalism of the traditional understanding of God and the world to one where transcendence becomes radically immanental, specifically the world is seen as within God and God is incarnated in the world. To see "transcendence become immanent" in the world, we will look at "wonder" (Mary-Jane Rubenstein), "adoration" (Jean-Luc Nancy), and "divine enticement" (Karmen MacKendrick). We will end the chapter with a suggestion of what difference the "inside" view makes when we consider the issue of "talking with trees" (Stephanie Kaza). Overall, this chapter is a study of the many differences that occur when our location is "inside nature" rather than the modern "outside view."

Wonder, Adoration, and Divine Enticement

From the challenging insights of Timothy Morton and Karen Barad on "where" we stand, we now turn to "what" we perceive, see, and hear from this new "inside" perspective. We will look briefly at the contributions of three postmodern thinkers who help turn our interest from supernaturalism to the wonder of earthly, human existence and to our responses of adoration and divine enticement. Until the last few decades, Western philosophy was principally focused on language, either the British variety of analyzing simple sentences of moral intention or the closed world of language (words refer to nothing apart from themselves). With the latter view, one could not talk about the world (and certainly not God), since language only referred to itself. However, there has been a turnabout in philosophy, especially European philosophy, and with some of these folks, "wonder" has returned. Hence what is going on in philosophy is of growing interest to theologians, with its concerns for both the beauty and the horror of existence. Philosophy has returned to its ancient partners—poetry and religion—and our next three authors move in this direction: Rubenstein and wonder, Nancy and adoration, and MacKendrick and divine enticement. Like Christian incarnationalism, this thinking focuses on the extraordinary as being located in the ordinary, not in spite of it or apart from it. This "new spirituality" is not about directing our attention to another world; rather, it is advising us to dig more deeply into this world. There is, therefore, a genuine opening for interpreting the doctrine of the incarnation more broadly—that is, not limiting it to one person, Jesus of Nazareth, but including the entire creation, human and beyond. The focus on the sacred in this world opens the doors for a kenotic theology where human beings work *with* God.

What Rubenstein, Nancy, and MacKendrick do is open the doors and windows of the world to encourage imaginative thinking about new metaphors and models of the relationship between God and the world. Each of these thinkers adds insight to the finite/infinite relationship. For all three of them, the self is only the self *in* relationship; hence "togetherness" is critical to the "self," and in fact, the Buddhist terminology of "dependent co-arising" describes ontology more accurately for them than anything in Western philosophy. In other words, "withness" is the essence of existence. Therefore, "kenosis," or self-sacrificial being, is the only existence there is—self-emptying love is not "added" to existence but defines it from the beginning. Here we see the connections with the life/death symbiotic pattern of evolution as well as the epitome of kenosis in the life and death of Jesus of Nazareth. In other words, the new worldview with its stress on interdependence is ideal for revising Christian theology in the direction of sacrifice and new life as the form of action that we find everywhere in the natural world.

The primacy of touch oversight expresses the centrality of "withness" for these authors. In another place, I have described this primacy in the following way:

> The first thing that mammals do with their newborns is to touch them. Animal mothers lick their young to form the bond necessary to their offspring's life. . . . Human beings can exist without their other senses, but we could not exist without touch: unless we are touched and can touch, we have no way of knowing that we even *do* exist—where, for instance, I begin and end, what is me and not-me. . . . If our understanding of the self, of who we are in the scheme of things, were to begin with touch (as our experience of actual selves does) rather than sight, we would have a *basically different sense of self*. Abandoning the Western

subject-object dualistic sense of self would reveal an ecological self, a relational self, a self that would not, could not exist apart from others. It would be a sense of self as relational and responsive. It would not be an individualistic self that decides to form relationships, but a responsive one that from its prenatal existence on is created by relationships. It would not be an abstract, rationalistic sense of self (I think, therefore I am), but a concrete, embodied sense of self (I am touched and touch, therefore I am).[1]

However, ever since Plato, sight has been the privileged faculty in human epistemology. As a consequence, the Western focus on sight over touch has allowed our knowing to be done from a distance, without touching—in fact, we can actually "hide" while seeing and not allow others to see us. Sight is the most distant of all our faculties, even hearing demands a speaker and a spoken to. As Rubenstein writes, "Thinking's (un)work is to get in touch with this chaotic touch of the world—and not, it cannot be emphasized enough, to hold itself above the fray. For unlike vision, which always collapses a perceived otherness back into the gazing self, touch exposes the infinitely inappropriable alterity between and within all beings, preventing the self's self-position." The "world is nothing except the touch of all things." Rubenstein speaks of "transimmanence," meaning the profound enfolding of the transcendent in the immanent. Thus the place of wonder (transcendence) is in the everyday (immanence). Rubenstein points to "the strangeness of the everyday," which opens up for us both the shock and the terror as well as awe and care. Thus while modernity kills wonder in its focus on technology, wonder breaks through to new possibilities, both negative (shock and terror) and positive (awe and care). Thus the relational network of touch that is our world is also the opening to a double possibility—"Shock unworks; awe makes sense."[2]

Hence Rubenstein's main focus, given its reliance on touch, is on the ethical, not the ontological. As a good Jew, Rubenstein focuses not on "belief" in God but on "love" to the neighbor. The law of hospitality thus rules her reflections: she mentions "saints" as people who practice "unconditioned hospitality," as epitomizing what she means by living the good life. She ends her book on learning how to breathe as the closest expression of "withness" or relationality: "Humanly speaking, air makes the self most properly itself; insofar as I breathe, I am no one else but me. At the same time, breathing opens the self *essentially* onto every other, taking in and releasing others and self and others-in-self-as-other at each moment. . . . With every exhalation, one sends oneself out into the lives of others, for better or worse." The last sentence of the book sums it up: "Perhaps that is it, then: perhaps dwelling in wonder is merely a matter of learning to breathe."[3]

From Rubenstein's "wonder" we move to Jean-Luc Nancy's "adoration," which is another attempt to move from a supernatural understanding of God to a view of transcendence as immanence. "The form of spirit as it awakens is adoration"—this quotation from Ludwig Wittgenstein opens Nancy's book and sums it up. It is a different step beyond Rubenstein's "wonder" in that Nancy attempts to substitute adoration of this world for the supernatural God. This sentence says that spirit awakens not to adore "God" but simply to adore what is—that is, our world. Nancy "deconstructs" Christian doctrines by giving transcendence totally immanental meanings. In the final paragraph of the book, Nancy speaks of Augustine's view of singing: he says it is to pray twice, and the second time it is simply a shout beyond all expectations—a hallelujah! salute from human beings and the chirping birds and thrumming cicadas: "Or again, the world saluting itself, via all of 'nature' up to 'mankind.'" It is a salute, a greeting, without salvation, without a god, without another world. As Nancy writes, "Adoration: the movement and the joy of recognizing ourselves as existents in the world."[4]

We are considering various attempts to reimagine transcendence and immanence, especially as a critique of present-day supernatural views of God, and also to consider proposals that find transcendence in our world. Would Nancy's position be just another form of atheism? One might think so from comments such as the following: "There is no other world, no world beyond"; "Adoration consists in holding onto the nothing . . . of the opening"; "The world, our world. Open to nothing other than itself. Transcendent in its own immanence."[5]

And yet, and yet . . . what does one make of the following: "This existence makes sense or *is* sense and with it the whole world can make sense from 'salut,' from one to another. Do not the morning sun, the plant pushing out of the soil, address a 'salut' to us? Or the gaze of an animal?"[6] "The gaze of an animal"—let us stop here and reflect on this. Nancy is asking us to relive those rare moments when one makes contact, real contact, with another species—that shocking, amazing experience of looking into the eyes of an animal and recognizing another subject, another living being with intentions and purposes. And furthermore, a "plant pushing out of the soil" is also, in its own way, a *presence making itself* felt. It is giving a "salute," a greeting, if one can pay close enough attention *and* open one's mind to an alive world. This is the uncanny effect of finding ourselves entangled with nature as an encounter with another living center of existence.

One of the most important insights from postmodernism is the expansion of our sense of agency, of who acts. It is summed up in the First Nations' reference to "all our relations," meaning all the life-forms in the world. It is an exercise in including more and more others within the parameters of our respect and moral concern, as subjects with agency who demand our attention and compassion. Nancy expresses it well: *the love that is owed to every existent simply because of its intrinsic worth*. In other words, love is justice, and love is a way of thinking; it is not merely a feeling. It is coming to the conclusion that nothing short of universal love is called for. From recognizing that something else really exists, that all life-forms have the right to the basics of existence, we have arrived at the "impossible" conclusion that there is no line of exclusion: all are welcome! Be careful what you pay attention to, with whom you "lock eyes, with what/who you believe is a 'subject.'" This is a cautionary tale: subjects do not always stay quiet or accept being considered as objects.

What is essential is this universal coexistence of all to all, the call and the response, the responsibility to respond each to each. How does this work out in terms of some central doctrines of Christianity? Evil consists in refusing to recognize that there is no singular "I" but only the "we" of life with others: "we are ourselves the relation among all beings" as we respond each to the other in self-giving love.[7] Sin is the condition of humankind closed in upon itself. Thus touching each other, sharing, greeting, caring for others: this is what is left. Nancy speaks of *creation* and *salvation*, the terms we used to reserve for what God did for us—now we do this for one another. But we are not alone: God is the "with" that empowers all this loving activity. Hence *revelation*, another Christian term, is not the revealing of some secret information but awakening to the *presence of the world*—the revelation is keeping the opening always open to the other. Moreover, the incarnation is "flesh itself as sense"—in other words, "the body is the event of the spirit," or "spirit does not hold itself outside the world, it opens in its midst."[8] Thus also, the resurrection is not a second life but the vertical life (the heavenly life) as made fully horizontal (realized in our world).

Nancy's interpretations of Christian doctrines are imaginative and engaging, but they ask a lot of us. Can we accept the substitution of this world for our former "two worlds"? He quotes a lovely passage from William Faulkner's novel *Requiem for a Nun*, where the central character says, "I believes" (not in something but just "believes"). What could this mean? Not believing that a Messiah will come to save us but simply adoring the "movement and joy of recognizing ourselves as existents in the world," which he compares to sexual ecstasy in the sense that it comes with the greatest shout of celebration that one could imagine: simply to be, to be here in all its beauty and horror, with the task of giving equality and justice to all.[9] Simply to be, to be here. Are we up to it?

Karmen MacKendrick proposes something different from Rubenstein or Nancy and more positive: "The world as the very sign of divine enticement."[10] We have been looking at various postmodern strategies for relating transcendence and immanence, ways that avoid supernatural, two-world thinking. We began with Rubenstein's call for us to wake up and stay awake to the wonders of *this* world, followed by Nancy's claim that "'God' is a name for the relation among all beings—therefore, [a name] for the *world* in the strongest sense of the word."[11] Now we come to MacKendrick, who, along with Augustine, speaks of "the world as the very sign of divine enticement."

We can see a progression here from waking up to this world to seeing this world as the sign, sacrament, symbol of the divine. Transcendence has not disappeared (except in its supernatural interpretation), but it has become embedded, incarnated, in this world, and we are called upon to "read" these intimations of transcendence in the world.

MacKendrick sees in Augustine's *Confessions* the form of "paying attention" that she supports. It is the classic Catholic, sacramental view where the world is rich with divine enticement in the form of all the loveliest things of this world. Augustine says, "Yet in a sense I do love light and melody and fragrance and food and embrace when I love my God— the light and the voice and the fragrance and the food and embrace in the soul, when that light shines upon my soul which no place can contain, that voice sounds which no time can take from me, I breathe that fragrance which no wind scatters, I eat the food which is not lessened by eating, and I love in the embrace which satiety never comes to sunder. This is that I love, when I love my God."[12] The world in its beauty calls out the name of its Creator, not in a simple or direct way, but through signs, which are seductive. From this network of signs, we get a sense of the divine as "within" and "around" the world: a sense of a call, a pull, that does not draw us out of the world but leads us more fully into it. Augustine's theology is significant because it sees the divine in the entangled complex that is the world. God "'dwells' in the world precisely as the perpetual invitation of and to our questions, our exploration, our delight."[13] The Word becomes flesh, not just mere words, and hence theology becomes "seductive epistemology," a kind of knowing that embraces even food and sex. The Augustinian world of signs is not a sterile, intellectual, spiritual, narrow world but the fullest, ripest, richest, most seductive one imaginable. MacKendrick claims that "the implication of reading the world as written by God is that the world reader is pulled by the reversible draw of divine desire."[14] God proposes; we respond. The power of this understanding of the God-world relation is that it believes in a God who is constantly inviting us, through each and every particular of the world (the lowliest slug included), to wake up, pay attention, and read God in the world—because God *is* in the world, or better still, the world is within God.

We have come quite a distance since Morton's claim that we human beings are "inside" the world to MacKendrick's claim, along with Augustine, that the *world is within God*. We have left the supernatural, dualistic world of modernism, trading it in for *one* world that is a sign of God. However, postmodernism is not just a return to the sacramentalism of Augustine. As a matter of fact, there are other postmoderns, influenced by quantum theory, who propose more radical embeddedness of the human being in the world than our sources have so far suggested.

Talking with Trees

If we accept our new standpoint as "inside" nature, along with all the other elements of nature, then we should feel "closer to trees"—in fact, close enough so we could "talk with them." If this does not strike you as absurd (or childish), then you have already made a big leap into the "knowing" and "doing" that is typical of postmodernism. There are several fine practitioners of this position: I would recommend to you the writings of both Richard Nelson (*The Island Within*) and Jane Bennett (*Thoreau's Nature*). After careful attention to Timothy Morton's insistence that the "ecological thought" is not about humans versus nature but about the radical interdependence of all forms of life, including the human form, as well as Karen Barad's undermining all dualisms, including subject versus object, perhaps now we can "talk with trees" without blushing. We have been focusing on the conceptual part of the new worldview; can we now ask, What does it feel like? Can we, for instance, imagine a biocracy as the proper form of planetary government that gives trees, mountains, birds, and even slugs "rights" to live and to flourish? Can we really include all others? Whose world is it, anyway?

One of the most important insights we have noted in postmodernism is its insistence that *the world is alive*. Therefore, we have to make a radical change. We can no longer assume that the world is composed of us, the one living subject, with everything else objects for our use. Now we must realize that the world is composed of many subjects with whom we relate in different ways. Part of coming to awareness of the relational quality of all life is to learn different techniques of being in relation with these many Others. One of the most important changes is to "feel" differently about them.

Stephanie Kaza, in her book *The Attentive Heart*, suggests that we practice a Zen form of meditation in which one's primary orientation to a tree is not as a symbol or resource but as a "Thou" (as Martin Buber would put it). This means that a tree can be seen as one party in an I-Thou relationship, not to speak "about" trees, but to speak "with" and "to" these Others. How can this occur without slipping into some sort of romantic consumerism, where in Morton's critique, we "consume" these Others into our own orbit or ego?

Kaza calls the needed practice "just sitting," being present with a tree as Other. Her stand toward trees is evident in the grammatical structure of the first sentence in her book: "The first tree to make my acquaintance as a child was the large-canopied apple tree in my backyard."[15] Notice that the *tree* initiates the relationship—the tree makes her acquaintance. She also speaks of trees as her "daily companions." She finds that over the years, her students have come "to see that the environment is everything. It is not just where we live; it is the very reason we are alive."[16]

This is the transformation that we need, that our new science is telling us is our reality—that without "nature," we would not even *be*. But it is crucial that we see our relationship with trees not in a sentimental way. We are not just "tree huggers," although a deeper appreciation for children's instincts of trees and other animals as "daily companions" is a good beginning. Why, I wonder, are almost all good children's books about animals? Is it because children "naturally" feel more comfortable with "them" than with members of their own species? Whatever is the case, most of us lose that sense of identification with other life-forms (and our culture encourages putting aside such "childish" attitudes). We have to practice what Kaza calls developing a "mutually respectful relation with trees." The crucial steps in this practice are as follows:

1. The first step is to recognize things *as they are*. A mountain is a mountain, a tree is a tree: *this* mountain, *this* tree. An aesthetic moment of appreciation for the other as having intrinsic worth and particular features is the first step. Compare it with God's view in Genesis after making each creature and feature in nature that it is good—not good for you (a human being) or even for me (God) but just plain good.

2. A second step is to look more deeply into the lives of particular trees, trees as both victims and shapers of human activities. Be specific: a good naturalist can spend pages describing in deepest details the habits of a particular kind of tree (for instance, the nature writings of John Muir).

3. The third step is to address the tangle of tree-human relationships—stories of fear, killing, suffering, exploding into waves of "despair, greed, and helplessness." Practice to deepen one's attentive mind from the insights of evolution and oneself as having a body made of flesh, even as trees also have bodies (different from ours) made of living matter.

4. In the last step, all this should climax in a greater, deeper internal consciousness and appreciation of trees so that one will make better decisions regarding trees in a time of horrible devastation of our planet's trees. The goal is a deeper conversation with trees, our "daily companions."

With the help of various readings from postmodern thinkers, we are trying to disorient and reorient ourselves in the world. Needless to say, this is an unsettling business. It doesn't always feel good: as Morton says, "Consciousness sucks." We are being asked to give up the comfortable, flattering picture of ourselves as at the center of the world and hence presumably in charge of things for a picture of ourselves in which we are not only decentered but among the most dependent and vulnerable of all creatures. On the other hand, this perspective and these practices open us to an *alive* world, full of other subjects with fascinating, diverse lives. At present, as the only subject, we live lonely lives in a seemingly dead world. We are being called to end living in a boring, consumer-oriented world, trading it in for a disorienting world, to be sure, but one interesting and alive, full of other subjects with intentions, practices, and gifts beyond any of our imaginings. We are being invited to really live in and with the rest of the world. Will we accept the invitation?

FOUR

God as Friend and
We as Friends of the World

As we have probed more deeply into the nature and breadth of kenosis, we have come to realize that it makes claims to be not only a way of knowing reality but also a way to live in it. As some critics have commented, "Only if kenosis is somehow in harmony with the ultimate character of reality should it be regarded as expected to be anything but foolishness."[1] We have shown it to be consonant with evolutionary science in its similarity in such notions as sharing, give-and-take, and the big one—new life is only possible through the death of others. Likewise, it is consonant with the heart of Christian theology— the action of the Trinity as one of constant receiving from one "person" and giving to another "person." Having established itself as critical to both science and religion—or more precisely, to evolutionary science and kenotic Christianity—we now wish to deepen our understanding of kenosis by suggesting that the model of God as friend is appropriate for divine action in a time of climate change. We will illustrate this by brief sketches of two kenotic theologies of friendship by Arthur C. McGill and Richard Kearney, both of them relevant to climate change.

Kenosis and the Model of Friend

Of the most central and powerful relational models for expressing the God/world relationship, "friend" is the richest and most suggestive. This may seem strange, since it is the least necessary when compared with parent or lover, as it does not have a biological base. As C. S. Lewis claims, "Rather, it is one of those things that give value to survival."[2] Since Aristotle, many have agreed with his comment "Without friends no one would choose to live even though he possessed all other goods."[3] And yet the reason for its superiority to parent and lover is a strange backhanded compliment. Lewis writes that one need not hesitate to call God Father or Husband because "only a lunatic would take such models literally. But if Friendship was used for this purpose we might mistake the symbol for the things symbolized."[4] In other words, "friend" is such an apt metaphor for God that it could be misinterpreted as a description!

Hence as a powerful candidate for expressing God's love for the world—as well as our response—it is composed, as Kant claims, of affection and respect and as such suggests that of all human loves, it "is the most free, the most reciprocal, the most adult, the most joyful, and most inclusive. Its range, from best friend to partner . . . reveals it to be eminently suited to participate in the formation of a new sensibility for the conduct of our public life and not just for our private pleasures."[5]

Kant's suggestion of affection and respect removes it from the intensity and potential individualism of parental love, where the parent's eyes are fixated on the child, or of lovers, where the lovers' eyes are obsessed with looking at each other. Rather, the friendship model suggests that God loves the world and all its creatures aesthetically—that is, loves each and every creature in appreciation of its uniqueness.

Friendship is the purest, most "disinterested" kind of love, appreciating each life-form in and for itself and what its diversity and specialness can contribute to the world. Likewise, with the friend model, we are called to love God because God is God and deserves our love—in fact, our adoration.

There are two places in the New Testament where the friend model appears: Matthew 11:19, where Jesus is seen as "a friend of tax collectors and sinners," and in John 15:12–15, where Jesus tells the disciples that they are no longer servants but friends and also claims, "No one has greater love than this, to lay down one's life for one's friends." Here we see boldly and clearly the kenotic motif, for *friends are called upon to sacrifice for others as the key to the life of discipleship*. Here we also see clearly the call of friends to face outward toward a common goal, and surely, the well-being of the planet is such a goal. While the parent looks at the baby and lovers at each other, friends join hands and face outward, united in a common interest. Here we see lifted up both inclusiveness and public concern: one can be friends with anyone, even nonsentient objects, such as mountains, libraries, gardens, and organizations. Likewise, while friendship can be seen as an exclusive model (my best friend), it can also refer to acquaintances who can join together regardless of gender, sex, skin color, nationality, disability, wealth, or poverty.

Yet for all its plaudits from secular sources over the centuries, friendship has a particular and high importance for Christians due to its centrality as a Trinitarian model. As Simone Weil puts it, "Pure friendship is an image of the original and perfect friendship that belongs to the Trinity and is the very essence of God."[6] Friendship is most fully expressed by an Eastern Orthodox interpretation of the Trinity. Rather than the Western individualistic substance view of the Trinity, the

Eastern relational dance-like view is both an illustration and an expression of kenosis. Unlike the Western view, which has encouraged radical monotheism (and hence we find individualism reflected in ourselves, the *imago Dei*), the Eastern view, underscoring the three "persons," helps us see God not as a static substance but as a constant activity of giving and receiving. The Trinity reveals that *to be and to be in relation* become identical, and hence there is no God outside the Trinity, and its characteristic is a constant giving and receiving in love.

Kenosis is not only best expressed by the model of friendship, but its typical ritual is table fellowship, the sharing of the basics (food, etc.) among all. While the Eucharist in the old monarchical story of Jesus fits with a substitutionary theory of the atonement—God in Jesus taking our sins upon himself, thus winning eternal life for us—here the bread and wine symbolize what "companions" (meaning "with bread") do. They eat together in order to renew their energy for working together for the well-being of the planet and all its creatures. The solidarity of friendship, its inclusivity and hospitality, is expressed in a kenotic view of the cross and resurrection as Jürgen Moltmann suggests in this comment: "It is the eating and drinking in the kingdom of God which the Resurrected anticipates with everyone whom he has made a friend."[7] To see the sharing of basic resources as a kenotic act in our time of climate change, with its consequences of dire inequality, is an essential commitment for us. It is a call to serious sacrificial action on the part of those humans who possess an unfair proportion of the planet's resources. *It is probably the most serious call to action that lies before us.*

Climate change also needs another characteristic of friendship—it is the most adult of all the God/world models. The model of God the Father, one of the favorites of Christians, keeps us permanently as "children," at most grateful to our all-powerful father but unable to contribute very much ourselves to the flourishing of the planet. Even the imperial models—lord, king, master, and so on—suggest our obedience, depriving us human beings of the responsibility that is rightfully ours, given that we are the only life-form able to *decide* to share the planet's resources. Hence in summary, the model of friendship between God and the world is especially powerful and appropriate as underscoring the adult nature of the relationship between God and human beings needed in our time. Let us recall John's comment suggesting our high calling in Jesus's remark that we did not choose him but that he chose us to love one another as he now loves us, not as servants, but as friends, laying down our lives for each other as he laid down his life for us (John 15:12–16).

From our analysis of the model of friend as primary for expressing the qualities of the God/world relation in a time of climate change—the qualities of inclusion, affection, respect, self-sacrifice, and partnership—we see the direction it is suggesting we go. The "direction" is toward "adulthood"—that is, taking our own lives and the condition of the planet with utmost seriousness. The two theologies that we will look at now are both "adult" theologies: they demand that we humans step up to the plate and play our role as the single most powerful species at present and the only one that can decide to live in different ways. In these theologies, God is calling us to assume our role as grown-ups in dealing with both the cause of and the response to climate change. We can no longer look to "Big Daddy" to save us from the consequences of our actions or protect us like children. However, this does not mean we are left on our own to solve the planet's problems. On the contrary, God calls us human beings "friends," surely an amazing and unexpected metaphor for both God and ourselves. As we have noted, friendship implies a "disinterested" affection and respect for the Other, recognizing the Other's intrinsic right to exist, quite apart from our need or desire. The basis of a relationship of friends is, then, the "well-being" of the other, even at some expense to oneself. Hence kenotic interpretations of Christianity as sacrificial love for others can be the "powerful" adult model of friends and partners needed in our time of climate change. Of course, the kind of "power" evident in kenotic Christianity is sacrificial love for others, a very different model of power from the one-way, unilateral, controlling power in traditional Christianity. Both Arthur C. McGill's "life by poverty" and Richard Kearney's "God after God" are instances of the strange "power" of weakness epitomized by Jesus's death on a cross—what is called "kenotic love."

By Possession or by Poverty

Arthur C. McGill, a Harvard theologian of a congregational bent, had a brief but stellar career during the middle of the twentieth century. He died young but had an impressive following. He is important to our subject of a viable Christian interpretation of the gospel for a time of climate change. He spelled out the heart of a kenotic theology with great economy, eloquence, and power. Several commentators speak of the risk that readers take when they read McGill. For instance, his opening salvo is "Have you ever realized that your death is the only thing in your life that is really yours?"[8] In another essay, he expands on this a bit: "My death is the climatic event of my own personal biography."[9] Why all this focus on death? First of all, simply because it *is* the most terrifying event on the human horizon, and to our knowledge, we are the only creature who lives with this information. Most religions are attempts to answer this human question about death, and in fact, popular versions of Christianity deliver a direct answer: Jesus's substitutionary atonement on the cross accepting responsibility for the sins of all human beings and thus assuring us of "eternal life."

But McGill does not let us off so easily. He claims that we humans are faced with two ways of living: by possession or by poverty, or life "on our own" versus life totally dependent on God and others. The life "by poverty," as one "totally dependent on God and others," is an excellent description of friendship, according to John 15:12–13: "This is my commandment, that you love one another as I have loved you. No one has greater love than this, to lay down one's life for one's friends." Here divine and human love are both described by friendship: unless we give up our life of false possession (sin), we will never experience real life, which is life from God and others. And as we recall, the "life of God" is the Trinity, where through reciprocal, sacrificial love, the never-ending activity of love moves the stars but also our planet and our own lives. So there is a surprising twist here: McGill claims that "death is the process of communicating life to others."[10] In a way similar to evolutionary theory, where new life is built upon the death of others, so with us, kenosis (self-sacrificial living) is the route to true life, both for oneself and for others. In the Trinity and in evolution, a similar pattern of kenotic, self-sacrificial love is central.

However, McGill is not talking about death in the biological sense; rather, he is asking us to die to our constant attempts to save ourselves, to have life on our own terms. This is the death he is concerned with: "Jesus does not die, period. He lays down his life to nourish us. . . . Therefore, to lay down the life we have already received, to lay it down that it may engender life in others, is not to die in the sense of being abolished; it is to die in the sense of generating life."[11] In other words, Jesus and his disciples must expend themselves, giving simply not from their excess but from the very marrow of their bones. One gives one's life, and according to evolution, a grain of wheat must die before it nourishes others. We must be transformed, take on a new identity, not the identity we possess now, but one that emerges from the give-and-take of the cosmic pattern of receiving and giving and never being independent. We must receive from God and others the nourishment we need for true living, our "ecstatic identity," which is identity received from others. Needless to say, this is a radically relational understanding of reality: it works by sharing, receiving and giving, dying and new birth; in fact, "I am" because "you are," and this means all the "yous" in the universe. So "loving the neighbor" is not just nice religious talk, but it is the way reality works.

Hence in this story of Christianity, Jesus "does not do it all"; rather, at all levels but in different ways, the pattern of new life depending on death holds. This being the case, we can never hope to live "on our own" by our possessions (whether wealth, reputation, or power); rather, we must accept our poverty, our neediness, and allow others to feed us as we must feed others. In other words, we must accept universal adult, reciprocal friendship—giving and receiving at deep, sacrificial levels, which holds at all levels of reality. Psychologically, we don't like this: we want to be the strong, independent "givers" to others (out of our excess) rather than being needy, dependent "receivers" from both God and others. McGill believes that the Christian churches have confused people by stressing what they can give rather than what they must receive: "In other words, what Jesus calls for is not for us to be unselfish, but for us to be empty, to be needy, to be, in ourselves, impoverished."[12] One of the most powerful ways McGill expresses this surprising twist is his analysis of the Good Samaritan parable. Most of us identify with the Samaritan (called "the good," who does excessive good deeds for someone else), but McGill claims the correct interpretation of the parable is that the reader is the needy one in the ditch and Jesus is the Samaritan giving life to the near lifeless.[13]

This is shocking—should not Christians love one another, share one's bounty, help others? McGill says yes, eventually, but first, we must give up trying to save ourselves through myriad ways: wealth, reputation, good works, and so on. He calls such people the "Bronze people"—folks who live in a dreamworld of success and cleanliness, health and beauty, perpetual youth. These folks pretend all is well, and McGill says of them, "I can't imagine where they carry their nightmares, their savagery, their decay and madness, their grief for all the suffering in the world."[14] The American dream of each individual competing with others to win the gold medal, or the corner office, is the sweet side of this way of living. The dark side appears in old age, when one's "possessions" have slowly disappeared. Old age is a lesson in nonpossession, where poverty becomes natural: the phone does not ring much any longer, one's appearance is crumbling, one's reputation is fading. McGill concludes, "Only at death are we purified of every strategy of being by possessiveness."[15]

The blessedness of poverty is that it generates empathy, awareness of universal "neediness," which is the heart of kenotic living: "If you reject need, you can neither give nor receive from one another, nor receive from God."[16] A remark by C. S. Lewis captures the essence of the pattern of receiving/

giving by means of the "game" that is played at cosmic, planetary, and personal levels:

> The golden apple of self-hood, thrown among the false gods, became an apple of discord because they scrambled for it. They did not know the first rule of the holy game, which is that every player must by all means touch the ball and then immediately pass it on. To be found with it in your hands is a fault: to cling to it, death. But when it flies to and fro among the players too swift for eye to follow, the great master Himself leads the revelry, giving Himself eternally to his creatures in the generation, and back to Himself in the sacrifice of the Word, then indeed the eternal dance "makes heaven drowsy with the harmony."[17]

We are now ready to go more deeply into our new life, the "ecstatic" identity, which means an identity we receive from outside ourselves. McGill writes, "Jesus' oddity lies in the fact that there is no moment when, to himself or before others, he is simply the reality which he possesses, simply his own self, so that a special shift of attention is necessary to be aware of God. In knowing himself, he knows the constituting activity of God as the constant and ongoing condition of his being. He never has his own being; he is continually receiving it."[18] He is similar to Augustine here: in knowing myself, I know God and vice versa. We are constantly receiving our very selves from God and others. McGill continues, "*We experience love.* . . . We experience this love primarily in terms of experiencing ourselves and in being ourselves. And when we experience ourselves as a gift, as a free, joyful, and continual gift, we are filled . . . with 'the feeling of gratitude.' . . . God is related to me constantly in every instant of my being. In being myself (which means in receiving myself from God's love) I feel gratitude as a basic and continuing feeling."[19] Here we are at the heart of the matter: real life, true life, is not the life we try to make for ourselves, on our own terms, a narcissistic life; rather, true life is what we receive moment by moment from others. This is not a spiritual, atypical religious experience; rather, it is gratitude for the most basic things in our ordinary lives. McGill further says, "We receive from God ultimately and from the world immediately. And we receive anew every morning. We receive all things anew—the air, our food, our friends, the world. And that is why it seems to me, for Jesus and for the New Testament, gratitude is always a fundamental feeling."[20]

Here McGill is being very Pauline: since one never "possesses" oneself, one need not be afraid of losing it. True freedom is now possible: having given up the fruitless activity of trying to save oneself, one can give liberally of oneself, for since each of us is fed by others (including God), one can live joyously and freely. However, a kenotic theology does not just involve receiving; each of us human beings must consciously make the decision to live in the universal pattern of receiving and giving (all other beings do so instinctively). It means life on the edge of a raft, for one never possesses oneself but must receive it constantly from others. As McGill admits, it is "a Shockingly Impractical Creed," for we are called to give our life in order to find it. We recall his interpretation of the Good Samaritan parable: the kind of love that Christ calls for is "essentially an activity of *self-expenditure* for another's need."[21] We cannot do this endlessly, hence McGill's interpretation that God is always the Good Samaritan and we are the needy ones in the ditch.[22] What McGill is pointing to is that the Christian life is not mere "imitating Jesus"; rather, *it is participating in God's own life, receiving self-sacrificial empowerment from the very being of God,* since we can never "love all the neighbors" on our own: "The life that Jesus brings is believed to be the *life of God himself.*" Jesus reveals not a mighty Lord but a self-expending friend. McGill explains, "If a man shares in the life of God, his real life will be found in *the act of offering himself in adoration to God,* and in obedience to God through service to his neighbors. The cross demonstrates that such offering involves a real *letting go* of the self. It involves dispossession, loss of identity."[23]

If Jesus reveals not a mighty lord but one of self-expending love, are we talking about gods? McGill defines the question more precisely when he says, "The question of the gods is nothing else but the question of power." And more specifically, the question of power brings up the issue of speech versus act. McGill again: "Jesus did not come to talk, but to die. It is the Word of God, not as an act of speech, but as a deed of self-expenditure and self-communication. For the deed entails what speech never entails. It implicates us as bodies, *it implicates our concrete actual life in the life of others.*"[24] McGill's understanding of power is incarnational; not only is God's power made known in weakness (after all, the "face of God" for Christians is a humble, itinerant carpenter), but our response to God's invitation to live a *new* life is profoundly embodied. As McGill writes, "God defines power, not power God."[25] This means that we must look to the story of Jesus to understand power in the new life. McGill writes that "Jesus exhibits a powerfulness that contradicts all our assumptions about power because in normal terms he seems utterly weak."[26] The difference is between power as dominating and power as nourishing, and "nourishing" in the ordinary sense of *feeding.* Taken all the way, incarnationalism means, first of all, *food for the body*. There is nothing romantic, spiritual, or merely verbal about this; rather, it is centered on *the deed of sharing life*. It is an act, and it is an act that involves self-expenditure, the *giving of one's own body* as Jesus gave his body to others. McGill sums it up: "I believe in God the nourisher almighty."[27] This certainly upsets all dominating versions of power with a phrase that initially seems almost foolish: "the nourisher almighty" (the "grand nanny"?). How awkward, how unimpressive, how weak! What has happened to all the glorious divine characteristics of Handel's "Hallelujah Chorus"—God the Lord of Lords and King of Kings?

Mention of the "nourisher almighty" brings us to the deepest way McGill expresses both our new life and our total dependence on God. He quotes John 6:56—"Those who eat my flesh and drink my blood abide in me, and I in them"—and then adds, "Since Jesus' death is essentially and literally an event of our nourishment, it can only be represented by eating and drinking."[28] How fortunate! This suggests that to understand the Eucharist, we look first at its literal meaning—it is a nourishing meal among friends. The common interpretation that the "flesh" and "blood" of Jesus is the price paid or punishment endured by Jesus to release us from our sins is the basis of the interpretation of the cross as substitutionary atonement. But what if we took it both literally (a meal among friends) and metaphorically (giving life to others)? This means that Christianity has profound appreciation for the basic necessities of life—food, shelter, clean air and water, education, and so on. *We should always keep in mind and return frequently to the table of friends sharing the basics of life.* This is the big picture and at the heart of Christian incarnationalism: the entire creation is loved and fed by God. The small picture, the process whereby this commitment is worked out in the world, is the giving of one's life for the well-being of others. He says very clearly that the evolutionary rule holds—in all eating at the animal level, some organism dies in the process of giving nourishment to another organism. In the following statement, McGill sums up the heart of the process and also its price: "Death is the final and inescapable mark of the communication of life. The person who loves his neighbors does not simply feel certain things. He concretely and willingly expends his aliveness for them. That is to say, he dies—if not today, then eventually. That is the inescapable truth. So far as he extends his energy, talents, and being toward the needs of others, he loses something of his own reality. In the end he will lose all of his present life."[29] The following brief comment contains both the prize and the price of loving others: "I am what I generate in others. My giving is my being."[30] One's gaining of true life, ecstatic identity from the very life of God, nonetheless takes its toll: one must let go of the life in oneself in order to pass it to others.

McGill's interpretation of the heart of Christianity is faith that true life comes from God and others and that this life is one of expending the self in the service of others. It is difficult to imagine a Christian theology where the model of friendship is more central according to John 15:13: "No one has greater love than this, to lay down one's life for one's friends." This is a summation both of Jesus's life and of the activity of the Trinity: self-sacrificial love among friends is the model of the God/world relationship we need facing the crisis of climate change. There are two critical characteristics of this model that are relevant: the cosmic dance of receiving and giving among "friends" (all the cosmic players at all levels). First, all the friends are "inside" the dance (including human beings), engaging as partners in the greatest show of all time—the evolution of planet earth. We believe also that this "show" has a tendency toward "love"; that is, the cosmic dance encourages all friends to give and take through the strange activity of self-sacrifice for others.

A Recovery of God after God

Kearney's book *Anatheism (Returning to God after God)* is a theological project that might be called a "covenantal process view without the metaphysics," or perhaps more accurately, with only intimations of metaphysics.[31] The ontological claim is there—God is coming, will come, can come, but only if we friends help God come, only if we hold up our end of the covenant by witnessing to the love and justice in the world. The relations between God and human beings are built on invitation and response, on possibilities the divine offers and our acceptance of these possibilities as our life vocation. Thus God and human beings are engaged as covenantal partners (or friends) for the well-being of the world. "If we are waiting for God, God is waiting for us," writes Kearney.[32] God is waiting for us not to become something but to do what Kearney calls the small things (that friends do for each other), like making sure friends have food and shelter or giving a cup of water to a thirsty person. This can be a beginning, an opening, that can lead to all sorts of other "kenotic" acts of sharing and sacrifice of various dimensions.

The reason Kearney is optimistic about us living this way is due not to us but to his understanding of God. He writes, "Such a divinity is 'capable' of making us 'capable' of sacred life, and it does so by emptying divine being into nonbeing [namely, us] so as to allow for rebirth into more being: life more fully alive."[33] Thus Kearney suggests that God's real

power is the divine empowerment of us (a kenotic understanding of power)—making us capable of being covenant
partners working with God for others. Thus while God may be
"weak," we are strong, and strong due to the divine power and
love being poured into us. This is what Kearney means by salvation: Jesus pouring out the divine life for others, culminating in the cross. So "the impossible [is] made possible," or we
receive what makes it possible that we can respond in kind.[34]

In *Anatheism*, therefore, Kearney is talking about not "the
death of God" in general but the death of a particular God—
the supernatural, distant God of ontotheology. *This* God must
die so that we can believe in God, the God of self-sacrificing
life. He quotes Meister Eckhart's prayer to God "to rid him of
God": "The God of religion, of metaphysics and of subjectivity
is dead: the place is vacant to the preaching of the cross and for
the God of Jesus Christ." Kearney claims that postmodernism,
with its critique of metaphysics and supernaturalism, allows
us to return to the tradition's deeper belief in the God of self-
sacrificial love for others. He mentions Dietrich Bonhoeffer's
claim that without such empowerment, his generation could
not have resisted the evil of Nazism. Kearney writes, "In short,
the death of God gives birth to the God of life. . . . To the weakness of the divine responds the strength of the human."[35] This
is not a new humanism—in fact, far from it; however, it is profoundly secular and worldly, for as Bonhoeffer says, only by
living completely in the world does one learn to have faith: "It
is not the religious act that makes a Christian, but participation in the sufferings of God in the secular world."[36] Unlike
humanism, this is kenotic, self-sacrificing life of the most radical kind. It is almost as if folks like Bonhoeffer are calling for
"a recovery of God after God." This is in no way a call for the
death of God, but it certainly is a call for a profound change in

how we live our lives, with Jesus Christ embodying the way. Christ offers us "his own personal life, in a second gesture of kenotic emptying (the first being the descent of divinity into flesh), so as to give life to others."[37] This is a radically different paradigm than the traditional Christology, which understands Christ's sacrifice as atoning for our sins.

Kearney summarizes the traditional view through its claim that the Eucharist is the church's celebration of Christ's work whereby we gain entrance into his atoning death by eating his body and blood. Kearney suggests differently, offering an "interpretation of Eucharistic embodiment as recovery of the divine within the flesh, a kenotic emptying out of transcendence into the heart of the world's body, becoming a God beneath us rather than a God beyond us."[38] Hence Kearney is suggesting a turn away from radical individualism, in which the "being" of both God and humans is an isolated existence, to a paradigm of "being" for both God and humans as "being-with," as friends. We are nothing apart from kenotic interdependence, but neither is God, as shown in the Trinitarian dance of self-sharing.

The incarnate God appears to need us in order to become fully embodied. Kearney has a healthy Catholic sacramental sensibility that sees God everywhere and especially in the despised, the small, the particular, the details. This kenotic Christology is nontriumphalistic; it is also a paradigm for us to follow as we answer when called: "Here we are." Needless to say, this understanding of God puts a large burden on us. Are we up to being friends with God? It certainly would be an "adult" role for us human beings to finally assume. For Kearney, however, God may appear to be powerless, but given his view of the incarnation in which the divine is emptied into creation, is not this immanence of divine love *the* source of the world's empowerment? However, Kearney's covenant between God and the world does demand our response: "The only Messiah still credible after the death camps would be one who wanted to come but could not because humans failed to invite the sacred stranger into existence."[39]

In summary, I find Kearney's brand of deconstructive theology deeply satisfying as a Christian and relevant to a time of climate change. He balances the two sides of Christianity—the Catholic, sacramental, incarnational (yes) side with the Protestant prophetic, covenantal, iconoclastic (no) side. Most deconstructionists work with the "Protestant" side; in fact, one could say that deconstruction (as the word suggests) is another version of Karl Barth's *Nein!* to all ideologies or Paul Tillich's protestant principle that denies absoluteness to any symbol. The no is easier to say than the yes, especially the appropriate, minimal, humble, small, kenotic yes. Christian faith, I believe, says both. What deconstruction reminds us is that our yes must be small and honest. Kearney adheres to this admonition, but he does say yes: we are invited to the feast, to the banquet, by the One who becomes embodied in us as we feed and clothe the least. A feast takes place as we help God be God. Thus the doctrine of "transubstantiation" of the body and blood of Jesus Christ into bread and wine for our consumption becomes the "transformation" of ourselves into capable partners serving the needs of the oppressed.

It is difficult for me to criticize this covenantal process theology, which has the marks of both Protestantism and Catholicism—a "sacramental return to the holiness of the everyday" that goes beyond most theologies of either kind in its metaphorical "seeing as," what Kearney called "mystical panentheism—the view that God is in all beings."[40] I find it personally relevant, scripturally sound, and a powerful motivator for acts of justice and love—including climate change—in its sacramental love of the world and prophetic call to save it. But are we up to it? Would not Augustine insist that we must already be "in grace" before we can respond; that is, God both calls for our help and must precede us in our answer as well, for we are powerless powerfulness on our own. A traditional Christian theology will say that grace enables us to answer; a metaphysical process view will say that God lures us with the possibilities that will fulfill us. Kearney seems to be saying that God knocks and knocks and knocks, hoping we will answer. Perhaps it is enough that—as Kearney says, quoting Mark 10—for us it is impossible, but all things are made possible by God. We can agree with that answer but still realize that we as friends have to open ourselves to that knowing. Some light is shone on this dilemma in another essay by Kearney entitled "Desire of God," where he suggests that our desire and our sense of responsibility are both traces of God— the urgings, if you will—that allow us to hear God knocking.[41] We need the traces—the stories, promises, covenants, and good works—that are the intimations of transcendence making it possible for our weak wills to open the door like adults to receive the empowering, kenotic love of God.

I will close on the note with which I opened my comments on Kearney. His God is the One before whom we can dance and sing and pray. This God is not the One who *never* comes but the One who is *always* coming, inviting us to "a morning that never ends." Kearney says,

> Let me end with a final eschatological image from the poetics of the Kingdom—the invitation to the feast. "I stand at the door and knock, says the Lord. If anyone hears my voice and opens the door, I will come in

and sit down to supper with him, and he with me." The great thing about this promise of an eschatological banquet is that no one is excluded. The Post-God of *posse* knocks not just twice but a thousand times—nay, infinitely, ceaselessly—until there is no door unopened, no creature, however small or inconsequential, oft out in the cold, hungry, thirsty, uncared for, unloved, unredeemed. The Post-God keeps knocking and calling and delivering the world until we open ourselves to the message and the letter becomes spirit, the word flesh. And what is this message? An invitation to the Kingdom. And what is the Kingdom? The Kingdom is a cup of cold water given to the least of these, it is bread and fishes and wine given to the famished and un-housed, a good meal and (we are promised) one hell of a good time lasting into the early hours of the morning. A morning that never ends.[42]

FIVE

Christian Theology in View of Kenosis, Theosis, and Postmodernism

In these closing pages, we will first look at three major reasons kenotic Christian theology is appropriate to deal with climate change. We will add some further reasons a postmodern kenotic view of the world is helpful at this time. First, we will analyze Eastern theology's understanding of salvation as "theosis" (deification), which equips us human beings for climate change.[1] We will then close with two brief sections: one on humanity's role in climate change and the other on God as the hope that we will need as we acknowledge that in the war on climate change, we are the "enemy."

Reasons We Need a Kenotic, Postmodern Interpretation of Christian Theology

The major reason that the traditional Christian story is not effective in dealing with climate change is that its assumptions, its worldviews, are out of date. No contemporary story is persuasive that does not accept the twenty-first-century worldview. In these pages, we have compared and contrasted the modern and the postmodern worldviews and found them very different. The problem with continuing to tell the Christian story in medieval or eighteenth-century, or even modern, assumptions is that they do not work when faced with today's problems. A religious story cannot be persuasive if it is too far from the science of its time, and for us, this means recognizing evolution and the sacrificial pattern to life that it embodies. We have tried to show that interpreting the Christian story in kenotic terms acknowledges the evolutionary reality that new life involves the death of others. While we see this pattern everywhere in nature, Jesus's self-emptying on the cross for others not only epitomizes the pattern but gives his disciples a way to live in a cruciform fashion by participating in God's own life. This story suggests not that we should "imitate" Jesus but rather that, like him, we gain our reality and our empowerment by participating in God's own life. This is why the Trinity as a reciprocal, continuous pattern of giving and receiving in an activity of love is central in Christian beliefs. We cannot live a self-sacrificial life on our own (even the saints do not claim to do so); rather, we must participate in God's own life of never-ending, empowering love to others. Kenotic Christianity is certainly not the only story that can be effective with climate change, but it is one version that is plausible in the twenty-first century. Human beings *must* have a narrative to live by, and they will hang on to a nostalgic, dated, ineffective story rather than have none. I am suggesting that telling the Christian story in a kenotic worldview is not only, I think, a highly persuasive interpretation of Christianity but also a plausible worldview when faced with climate change.

The second big reason that the traditional Christian story must be reinterpreted in kenotic and postmodern terms is that while the traditional story centers on individuals, the kenotic, postmodern interpretation is radically relational. Unfortunately, many contemporary Western worldviews are intensely individualistic. When we imagine "humanity," we think not of a community but of the Western hegemonic individual who is male, white, educated, well-off, fit, and trim. We praise these individuals who make it against the odds but have scant concern for the millions who need a security net. Eighteenth-century Enlightenment assumptions about the value of the individual were a real gift of interpretation in contrast to the medieval worldview that buried the individual beneath hierarchies and myths. We postmoderns have greatly benefited from the Enlightenment's rescuing of the individual as being significant. Women especially have benefited, but all human beings should be grateful for modernity's focus on the rights of the individual. But this focus—which has become an obsession, with the narcissistic emphasis on the "self"—is now out of date, though the social media folks have not yet acknowledged it.

The postmodern view is the polar opposite of the modern one. At a time when climate change is the biggest challenge facing the world, we need the holistic, radically relational, interdependent, communal view. The first criticism by postmoderns of modernity is its absurd belief that the individual can exist alone. From our beginnings in our mother's womb, where we are totally dependent on her (and those who protect and feed her), we are never alone. In fact, the umbilical cord is a metaphor for our entire lives: we are microscopically and macroscopically dependent on the planet and all its resources and systems. To be free of the planet for even a minute endangers our lives, for our very next breath depends on our immersion in the planet. Our independence would be a "joke" if the assumptions accompanying it were not so dangerous.

They are dangerous because they give us the myth that we can live well even as the planet deteriorates from our overuse of its resources, especially fossil fuels. The very things we need now—a deep gratitude for the gifts of planet earth and our willingness to do everything possible to keep it healthy—cannot be based on the myth of individualism. In fact, we need to practice "radical relationality." Anything that helps us think in those terms, any story that assumes the interdependence of all life-forms—and helps us incarnate that in our minds, our emotions, and our actions—is valuable. In a fashion similar to the way we have internalized "individualism" in our thoughts and practices, we need to embody radical relationality. Fishes in the sea? Babies in the womb? The roots of a tree? An origami? We need to imagine ourselves with these images.

And this comment brings us to the final big reason we need to change our story in a kenotic, postmodern mode. It is our "standpoint": Are we "outside" or "inside" nature? This is probably the most difficult change we need to make. As long as we continue to imagine ourselves as "outside" reality, we will cling to a subject/object epistemology, which invariably places human beings in the top position. We are the "subjects," looking at and down at the rest of our planet as "objects" either useful or not to human beings. We will never make much progress with climate change until we recognize it as a powerful player (subject) in our planet's nature and future.

Timothy Morton's lifework is how to move people from our imagined standpoint outside and above the planet to our rightful place radically within the planet. Just because we can imagine ourselves somewhere else doesn't mean we actually inhabit that place. Our imagination—the potential to create worlds in our minds—is one of the distinctive features separating us from other animals. However, this does not mean we are superior to other animals or that the planet should do our bidding. One of the most attractive and viable models for the divine/human relationship is to imagine us as living "within" God. God is not over us, separate from us, but God is still "more than" we, who live completely "within" God, are. This model is attractive because it is incarnational, communal, radically relational, and it reminds us of the mother's womb, which is a model of radical dependency, as well as of warmth and security.

So these are the three big reasons kenotic, postmodern theology is a fit worldview for facing climate change: it is consonant with the science of the day, it encourages radically relational thinking and acting in all circumstances, and it insists that our proper standpoint is "inside" the planet with a glimmer of "outside," given our imaginations. One of the tasks of theology is to monitor the interpretations of Christianity for one's time. I am saying loud and clear that the modern Christian story—built as it is on the primacy of the individual, as well as its dualistic, hierarchical, patriarchal models of the God/world relationship—is a false and dangerous one. It not only encourages male, hierarchical, dualistic behavior on the part of human beings (as in present-day capitalism), but it is also a devastating model for the planet, since it encourages reckless resource development.

There are as well many other reasons postmodern thinking is appropriate for dealing with climate change. Perhaps the most important of these reasons for religious discourse is a central feature of postmodern thinking: its return to wonder and awe. It helps move transcendence out of the sky and onto the earth. The postmodern sense of immanental transcendence is a reminder to the Christian community of its sacramental tradition. Rather than two static beings, one on earth and one in heaven, postmodernism imagines the divine as incarnated, on the same earth that we walk every day. The world is alive: it is a wondrous place microscopically (the complexity of a beetle's anatomy) and macroscopically (the number of stars in a night sky). It is composed not of mechanistic-like atoms but of billions of subjects that affect us and the planet every minute. Thus the child's readiness to talk with trees and to anthropomorphize other animals is not primitive or wrong. Rather, it is probably more "right" than the modern relation to a forest as "how many board feet" it contains.

It means, further, that with this image of "aliveness" in mind, we are more able to understand "agential realism," or the inclusive and complex forms of agency that we meet on the planet. Perhaps we will also be more willing to accept responsibility for "natural" events, such as the increasing frequency and strength of hurricanes and floods in our time of climate change. Perhaps we can assume a more humble position for ourselves on the earth, not claiming we know everything or can fix anything, but listening to those who spend many years studying an event, as well as "listening" to the planet itself. One of the gifts of postmodernism is its insistence that there are no dualisms, only continuities, in nature. Thus we need no longer separate out the human community into rigid races and sexes. We postmoderns celebrate "differences," not dualisms: there are no black or white people, only folks along a continuum of color. Likewise, human beings aren't entirely male or female; rather, there are many notches on the sexual line.

Hence the various insights from postmodernism return us to where we began—it is touch, not sight, that is our basic faculty. We do not stand back and survey the world at our beck and call; rather, we grope our way out of the womb and into planet earth gradually, first by touch. We start putting our world together, one foray after another, eventually exchanging touch for hearing and sight—more abstract, less embodied ways of knowing. But we never leave our profound reality as embodied and are not only happier when we are in a touching relationship with the planet but more likely to respond wisely and effectively to climate change when we know and love our planet from the "inside."

Deification as the Goal of Human Life and Climate Change

Deification, or participation in God's life, makes it possible for us to be empowered by God as we face the challenge of climate change. However, this topic sounds odd to "Western" ears, where the goal of human life or salvation is usually focused on Jesus assuming all the sins of the world and receiving punishment for them (death on a cross), while we humans are let off free. The "Eastern" view is considerably different in several ways. First, there are two stages to salvation in Eastern theology: kenosis and theosis (deification), whereas the Western view usually stops with the cross and the atonement. Deification involves human participation, since we too must live kenotic lives—even as Jesus went to the limit to manifest his sacrificial love for the world, so we are called to live similarly for our "neighbor" (the planet). Here we have two stages in salvation: a first one of cruciform love and a second of deification, living by participation in God or in friendship with God. In Western salvation, there is only one stage, a "negative" one in which our sins are removed. The extra stage in Eastern thought allows for a joyous, intimate relationship with God because we cannot live "as God does" unless we participate *in* God. In fact, Eastern theology has various ways to express theosis: imitation of God, taking on God's nature, indwelt by God, being reformed by God, being conformed to Christ, the final divinization of the cosmos.

A second difference in Eastern thought is its basic theology serving as the environment for Christology. As Mark A. McIntosh expresses it, right living or deification is "a rediscovery of *reality as participation in divine communion*."[2] To this way of thinking, reality is always a participation in divine communion, including creation, the incarnation, and discipleship. Hence creation is not "out of nothing," but "in creation, God gives of himself." Likewise, the incarnation is, like creation, based on the nature of God. Lucien Richard says, "Creation and Incarnation are the results of a movement of divine compassion in the very heart of God"—in other words, the Trinity.[3] Irenaeus points to the grand exchange, in which, as Athanasius puts it, he became human that we might become Godlike.[4] The goal of all God's works (creation, incarnation, the cross, etc.) is so we might become companions, friends, with God! This is amazing when contrasted with the goal of traditional Western theology: the divine pardon of human sins. But here the goal of all God's works is for the sole purpose of friendship with God. As McIntosh states, right living is "practicing what it is like to know the world in companionship with God."[5] From such a perspective, life is a journey of discovery toward deeper participation in God's own life. Pierre Teilhard de Chardin captures it well in this prayer when he perceives he is dying: "And above all at that last moment when I feel I am losing hold of myself and am absolutely passive within the hands of the great unknown forces that have formed me; in all those dark moments, O God, grant that I may understand that it is You (provided only my faith is strong enough) who are painfully parting the fibres of my being in order to penetrate to the very marrow of my substance and bear me away within Yourself."[6] Hence even at the moment of death, the Christian knows his or her very death occurs within God; in fact, eternal life means God parting the fibers of one's being to welcome all to the total participation in God's own life.

A third difference between the Western and Eastern views of salvation is the substance of salvation. Michael Gorman sums it up nicely with his phrase "cruciform theosis," which can be used to describe both God and human beings: "Kenosis is thus the *sine qua non* of both divinity and humanity, as revealed in the Incarnation and Cross of Christ, the one who was truly God and became truly human."[7] This similarity between God's life and our own means that the same pattern of kenosis first and then theosis is followed. In other words, God in Jesus Christ does not "do it all" (save us); rather, just as God's life is counterculturally kenotic, so our lives should be also, not so much by imitating God in Christ, but by *participating* in God's own life. It is here that we both know what to do (love kenotically) and also gain the means to do so; that is, on our own, we cannot fulfill the commandment to love the neighbor kenotically (with self-sacrificial love), but participating in God's own kenotic love allows us to do so. Or as Paul Gorman says, "Therefore to be truly human is to be Christlike, which is to be Godlike, which is to be kenotic and cruciform."[8] Here we have a summation of the divine and human lives, which are more similar than different! Paul had an "Eastern" view of salvation: "I am crucified with Christ: nevertheless I live; yet not I, but Christ liveth in me" (Gal 2:20 KJV). Here we see what the Christian life is meant to be: living in radical dependence on God, not only for one's next breath, but also for the empowerment to fulfill the commandment to love the neighbor as oneself.

The old story—the story of the sovereign, all-powerful God in heaven who took upon himself in Jesus Christ the sins of all human beings so that we could live forever with God in heaven—has a happy ending. Most people do not believe this crude version of the story, but its important points, such as an all-powerful God living in another world and doing everything necessary to save us, are widespread. Some version of that story—a supernatural Power that will save us—lies behind many modern people's beliefs. It is a comforting story, while the kenotic version demands effort all around (by God as well as us). So why not continue with the old story? The main reason is that it is no longer credible, given what science tells us about our world. It is for this reason that I have outlined the many parts of the postmodern understanding of reality. Fortunately, as we have seen, the postmodern worldview fits very well with a kenotic theology—better than the modern view focused on the individual. In fact, the postmodern view is almost the opposite, resting as it does on radical interrelationship. As a Greek physics scholar, Argyris Nicolaidis, puts it, "The whole of nature . . . appears *strongly interrelated*, forming a unique and coherent entity, to which we belong and remain in constant interaction." In fact, postmodernism is so focused on relationality that Nicolaidis substitutes for the Cartesian subject (who exists because he or she thinks) the phrase "I relate, therefore I exist." This is the key to postmodernism, and it is difficult to overstate its importance, particularly at the quantum level, where Nicolaidis comments, "Although a complete overall picture is not available, it is quite clear that we should avoid the old dualisms, the dissociation of matter from energy, and placing subject and object in opposition."[9] It is not necessary that theologians need to know the latest twist in postmodernism ontology and epistemology. It is, however, necessary for theologians to work with the basic worldview of our time; otherwise, the story of our faith will not be credible, nor will it be effective against climate change.

So where does this leave us? We have accepted the fact that, in the kenotic story, we human beings participate in our salvation, even to the point of the cross. John Zizioulas comments that the new story, focused as it is on relation to the other, demands cruciform living from us:

> Communion with the other requires the experience of the *Cross*. Unless we sacrifice our own will and subject it to the will of the Other, repeating in ourselves what our Lord did at Gethsemane in relation to the will of his Father, we cannot reflect properly in history the communion and otherness that we see in the Triune God. Since the Son of God moved to meet the other, his creation, by emptying himself through the *kenosis* of the Incarnation, the "kenotic" way is the only one that befits the Christian in his or her communion with the Other—be it God or one's neighbor.[10]

These sentences sum up very clearly the position of the Christian. It may sound daunting, but if we are called to participate in God's own life, then the self-giving love we see in the Trinity defines the God we are called to follow. According to Richard, "In the cross we discover the fundamental law of the divine life itself: 'Power is to be found in weakness.'"[11] As we have seen, this is not meant as a conundrum to confuse people; rather, it is insisting that the same process that we see in evolution, where some sacrifice for others, has been taken by God as the sine qua non of both God's life and ours. But we are not alone—to be sure, we are called to self-giving sacrificial love for the benefit of others (especially those of us who are well-endowed with possessions, power, and influence), but by answering this call, we are participating in God's own life.

Hence there is hope—God's life includes a resurrection as well as a cross. In fact, one could say that *transcendence* means "hope," that it means "possibility." As John Caputo puts it, "Transcendence is the insistence or the promise of the world."[12] Other words Caputo uses for *God* are "love," "gift," "justice," "hospitality," and "grace." Or "God" means that there are possibilities. And as we face the reality of climate change, hope or possibilities is the one thing we need to hear. Kenosis, self-giving love, is the right kind of empowerment for human beings. We now know that we can't control or conquer nature, but we *can* answer the call of God to join in the practice of self-emptying so that God's love can empower us. The doctrine of the incarnation makes divine possibility possible because Jesus is "the face of God" for Christians. Hence we know from the story of Jesus what we well-off human beings should be doing. A practice of "minimalism" is probably wise. We cannot save the world, but we human beings—who know what we are doing to the planet and its poorest creatures, both human and otherwise—can change our ways. With a revised story of our faith, one that is consonant with the twenty-first century, and by participating in the very life of God as partners and friends, we are not left alone to sit in the mess we have created on our planet. Rather, God is with us, or more accurately, as Augustine pointed out, we live "within God" whether we live or die. Hence we should not lose hope. This may not be the "salvation" we are used to (God doing everything for us), but it is a call to move out of infancy (God as father) to an adult relationship (God as partner and friend).

Humanity's Role in Climate Change

Humanity's role should be one of (1) respect and affection for nature, (2) an adult partner role, (3) a role that for some human beings will be self-sacrificial.

A postmodern worldview radically changes our standpoint from one of superior sovereignty or infantile helplessness to one of respect (for other subjects) and affection (for our kin). We human beings have a complex relationship with nature. On the one hand, we owe our very lives to Mother Nature, including our next breath. On the other hand, human beings, through our excessive and thoughtless behavior, have actually caused what we rely on totally to disintegrate and be unable to support our population's needs and desires (let alone support the rest of nature).

Given our dependency on and power over the natural world, our first response ought to be respect for the "otherness" of nature. Just as we should recall God saying in Genesis after each creation of sun, water, flora, and fauna, it is good—not good for humans or even me, God, but good in itself. In other words, God's first reaction to the creation of various aspects of nature, then, is an aesthetic, appreciative one. Natural systems and life-forms are intrinsically good and ought to be valued as "subjects" that have intentions and agency of their own, regardless of their usefulness to human beings. In addition to respect, we ought to feel affection for the trees, water, fish, mammals, and so on as "kin." The evolutionary fact that everything on the planet has the same roots means that we are related to the rest of nature as either close or distant relatives. Thus the First Nations' address to nature as "all our relations" and the child's habit of imagining other animals as friends with whom one can have a conversation are both on the mark. These attitudes of respect and affection are much more appropriate than the modern stance since Descartes's of separating out human beings as the only live subjects while the rest of nature are objects for our use.

Second, if we manifest respect and affection for nature, we will be dealing with it in an "adult" way. We are more likely to imagine nature in terms of a partner or friend than as our playground or department store. If we see nature as partner and friend, then the various traits of a friendship pertain. We would meet nature as adults who recognize the "other" as a subject with intentions and value. We would no longer either rest nostalgically in the warm arms of nature or use nature for our excessive desires but approach it as a valued friend. We are bound to use some images with which we approach nature, so let's head for an adult relationship where we deal with nature in terms of its own needs and ways of action. Thus we would pay close attention to the images and concepts from scientists: evolutionary and quantum theories both provide important information for any person or group attempting to work fairly and fruitfully with nature. The climate change deniers are the enemy of nature because they refuse to approach nature scientifically, similar to the tobacco deniers' refusal to acknowledge current science on smoking. Nature is neither our plaything nor our slave but our "other" who demands we meet her or him with adult appreciation and objectivity.

Third, if we assume the attitudes already named, then we will also realize that some of us must approach nature in a self-sacrificial mode. The relationship is not "human beings and nature" but *some* human beings and nature, those with significant money and power to pull back their desires that are taking an unfair percent of nature's bounty, leaving other life-forms destitute. Currently, the planet's riches are divided in a grossly unfair fashion, with the top 2 percent or so owning most of the planet's resources. Unfair distribution means the planet cannot flourish unless all of the parts flourish. Sadly, the attitude by the wealthy of selective self-sacrifice is far from being widely practiced, and governments are shy about legislating it. Most Westerners and many Christians are repelled by the notion of sacrifice. Many Westerners, especially Americans, are firm believers in the "religion" of consumption and live to shop! Some Christians claim "Jesus sacrificed for us," so we do not need to do so. But from our analysis of kenotic, postmodern living, it is the posture that many human beings should assume. It is the appropriate standpoint for all well-off human beings, but it is even more necessary for Christians who claim to be disciples of Jesus, for whom cruciform living was the center of his existence—and whose commandment to his disciples was to love your neighbor as yourself.

Hence we have sketched a role for human beings in regard to climate change that is refreshingly adult, objective, and "real." It does not assume that we human beings can control climate change, on the one hand, or that we have no role to play, on the other hand. On the contrary, it suggests we meet nature as adults—friends, relations, and partners—in this glorious experiment of life on planet earth.

God's Role in Climate Change

It is perhaps absurd to speak of "God's role in climate change." God does not have "roles" to exercise; rather, God *is* hope. The one thing that we need as we sit despairingly in the shit we have made of the planet is some hope that the situation is not hopeless. As climate change becomes more real and closer to home (hurricanes Harvey and Irma), we wonder what can be done. It is easy to become apocalyptic and to "give up." It used to be that the "weather" was a safe topic for casual discussion, but it is fast becoming a "hot topic," too divisive for polite conversation. This is because the "weather" (understood as climate change) has become a terrifying subject, pushing aside sex, money, and religion as the untouchable topic.

Nonetheless, the postmoderns who are reluctant to use the word *God* are replete with substitute words. Caputo's "transcendence is the insistence or the promise of the world" means that there are possibilities, worldly possibilities, because "transcendence" is not out there but here, incarnationally in the world. For these folks, "transcendence" means hope, possibilities, radical immanence, love, justice, hospitality, gift. Caputo puts some meat on these bones when he writes, "Faith thus means faith in more life, in life/death, in the grace of the moment, of the hour, of the day, of the life-time. . . . We love life because we love the rain on our faces even as we also love sunny days. . . . We love life because life is life, because we love life, and this tautology, by saying the same, says everything. Loving life is our best theory of everything."[13]

With their insistence on immanental transcendence, postmoderns are being good "incarnational" Christians, emphasizing the world as the place of God's habitation. Hence the "power of God" is also worldly; it is the empowerment of us human beings so we can befriend our planet, helping us meet the challenge of climate change as adult partners. God is not the all-powerful divinity that will "conquer" climate change; rather, power is to be found in weakness, or as

Richard comments, "Divinity consists supremely and essentially in self-giving and letting-be," both characteristics of friendship.[14] In other words, we can never conquer or control nature, but we *can*, through our deification or participation in God's life, practice self-emptying so that God's loving friendship can work through us and we can become channels of justice and hospitality.

This does not mean that we will be "successful" in our work on climate change. At most, we can do small acts embodying the friendship of God in our efforts toward planetary hospitality, justice, and compassion, manifesting God's love for the world. We say the big words (friendship with the planet) and do our small acts: the big word is Julian of Norwich's "all things shall be well" (a cosmic vision of hope and possibility), which is God's word, and we practice Dorothy Day's "little way," the minimalism of Day, who wrote that she did nothing outstanding, but she persevered: "She claimed that her work did not require great talent but mostly hard work: 'I have done nothing well, but I have done what I could.'"[15]

But the saintly way is not the only way or even the best way for most. Christianity is not mainly a practice by individuals of kenotic empowerment. Rather, the parables of Jesus and his life and his death on a cross suggest something else—the kingdom of God as a countercultural way to live. While Christianity is not a blueprint for a new society, it is meant both as a new worldview in which the standards of the world are inverted and as a call to live now as a kenotic community of friends.

I would like to close this book with some thoughtful words from Barry Lopez in his fine book *Arctic Dreams*. It is a passage I find illuminating as we face the challenge of climate change:

No culture has yet solved the dilemma each has faced with the growth of a conscious mind: how to live a moral and compassionate existence when one is fully aware of the blood, the horror inherent in all life, when one finds darkness not only in one's own culture but within oneself. If there is a stage at which an individual life becomes truly adult, it must be when one grasps the irony in its unfolding and accepts responsibility for life lived in the midst of such paradox.... There are simply no answers to some of the great pressing questions. You continue to live them out, making your life a worthy expression of a leaning into the light.[16]

This is the time when we well-off human beings are being called to be "truly adult," facing the dilemmas of climate change with objectivity, honesty, and compassion—the qualities of a friend to nature in need.

Afterword

A Reflection on Kenosis and Christianity

Kenosis (or self-emptying) is central to Christology, God, creation, and us. It is a totally different view of reality than either the medieval or Enlightenment pictures of who God is and who we are. It is also key to the only way to live on our planet, where evolution is semikenotic in its sacrifice of old life for new life. Kenosis is a different way to be in the world in every conceivable way. For instance, the old story of Christianity is a negative tale of sin and redemption. It is about two solitary individuals—God and the human being—who have gotten out of sync with each other and need to be reconciled. This reconciliation occurs through the substitutionary atonement of Jesus Christ for the sins of all human beings—past, present, and future—so that God is no longer angry at the world gone astray. God's honor has been saved by the sacrifice of Christ's life. Our role in this story is to "have faith" that Jesus Christ has indeed saved us. Our gratitude is shown by acts of mercy to less fortunate people.

A kenotic view, however, is entirely different: it claims from the outset that God loves the world and that its life is grounded by participation in God's own life. This story is first of all positive. It is about the incredible intimacy of all things in God. Indeed, "reality" here is participation in God's life and love. No individuals can exist alone at any level; reality is relational, all the way from the Trinity itself (which is solely an activity of love) to the glimmers of sacrificial activity in evolution. Kenosis claims that "living" is totally interrelational and interdependent; thus Christianity is not first of all a negative story about human sin, but it is a joyous, celebrative story where God in God's self (the Trinity) is the epitome and the finest expression of kenosis: the act of receiving and giving, sacrifice and new life, reciprocal interdependence, that is the heart of how our universe operates.

Christianity fulfills kenosis. It claims that the only way to live fruitfully and responsibly on planet earth is to follow the planet's "house rules": take only your share, clean up after yourself, and leave the planet in good repair for Christians. The story of Jesus is, for Christians, the best entry into this story. The kenotic story of Jesus opens up the following topics: who Jesus is, who God is, what creation is, and who we human beings are. It is a total story of who we are and what we should be doing on planet earth. It is a beautiful, awesome, and challenging story, which we human beings, the only self-conscious creatures on our planet, are invited to join.

If we do not join this cosmic, relational dance, we will not only be living outside of "reality," but we will be miserable, since fulfilled life is not possible outside of this circle. The old monarchical tale of sinners alienated from God and the world is, by comparison, negative and limited, pertaining principally to the forlorn side of human beings while ignoring most of creation as well as the joy of living in love with the rest of creation. The story of reality is a stunning, almost unbelievably complex, diverse panorama of beauty and richness, as well as sharing and sacrifice, to which each of us is invited to join for a few years.

Notes

Prologue

1   Annie Dillard, *Pilgrim at Tinker Creek: A Mystical Excursion into the Natural World* (New York: Bantam, 1975), 2.

Introduction

1   Yuval Noah Harari, *Sapiens: A Brief History of Humankind* (Toronto: McClelland & Stewart, 2014), 31.
2   George F. R. Ellis, "Kenosis as a Unifying Theme for Life and Cosmology," in *The Work of Love: Creation as Kenosis*, ed. John Polkinghorne (Grand Rapids, MI: Wm. B. Eerdmans, 2001), 108.
3   Lucien J. Richard, *A Kenotic Christology: In the Humanity of Jesus the Christ, the Compassion of Our God* (Lanham, MD: University Press of America, 1982), 170.
4   Holmes Rolston, "Kenosis and Nature," in Polkinghorne, *Work of Love*, 49, 50, 56.
5   Rolston, 52.
6   Rolston, 54, 52.

7 John D. Zizioulas, *Communion and Otherness: Further Studies in Personhood and the Church*, ed. Paul McPartlan (New York: T&T Clark, 2006), 5–6.

8 Richard, *Kenotic Christology*, 133.

9 Jürgen Moltmann, *The Crucified God: The Cross of Christ as the Foundation and Criticism of Christian Theology* (New York: Harper & Row, 1974), 204.

10 Moltmann, 205.

11 John D. Caputo, *The Weakness of God: A Theology of the Event* (Bloomington: Indiana University Press, 2006), 33.

12 Michael J. Gorman, *Inhabiting the Cruciform God: Kenosis, Justification, and Theosis in Paul's Narrative Soteriology* (Grand Rapids, MI: Wm. B. Eerdmans, 2009), 161.

13 As quoted by Jeffrey Finch, "Irenaeus on the Christological Basis of Human Divinization," in *Theosis: Deification in Christian Theology*, ed. Stephen Finlan and Vladimir Kharlamov (Eugene, OR: Pickwick, 2006), 86.

14 Thomas Merton, *New Seeds of Contemplation* (New York: New Directions, 1972), 159.

15 For instance, for an analysis of saintly action, see my book *Blessed Are the Consumers: Climate Change and the Practice of Restraint* (Minneapolis: Fortress, 2013).

One: The Kenotic Stories of Jesus and God

1 Richard, *Kenotic Christology*, 175–76.

2 Richard, 315.

3 Teresa Kuo-Yu Tsui, "Seeing Christian Kenosis in the Light of Buddhist Sunyata: An Attempt at Inter-faith Hermeneutics," *Asia Journal of Theology* 21, no. 2 (2007): 364.

4   Richard, *Kenotic Christology*, 211.
5   For a discussion of "although" versus "because" in this critical place, see Michael J. Gorman, "Although/Because He Was in the Form of God," chap. 1 in *Inhabiting the Cruciform God*.
6   McFague, *Blessed Are the Consumers*, 8.
7   Gorman, *Inhabiting the Cruciform God*, 161.
8   Michael J. Gorman, *Cruciformity: Paul's Narrative Spirituality of the Cross* (Grand Rapids, MI: Wm. B. Eerdmans, 2001), 92.
9   See the discussion of these two approaches to the Trinity in the theology of Zizioulas, *Communion and Otherness*, 237.
10 David H. Jensen, *In the Company of Others: A Dialogical Christology* (Cleveland: Pilgrim, 2001), 29–30.
11 Richard, *Kenotic Christology*, 310.
12 Richard, 211.
13 Richard, 180.
14 Richard, 84.
15 Wesley Wildman, "An Introduction to Relational Ontology," in *The Trinity and an Entangled World*, ed. John Polkinghorne (Grand Rapids, MI: Wm. B. Eerdmans, 2010), 55.
16 Zizioulas, *Communion and Otherness*, 210–11.
17 Zizioulas, 211n9.
18 Vladimir Lossky, *The Mystical Theology of the Eastern Churches* (London: James Clarke, 1957), 65.
19 Kallistos Ware, "The Holy Trinity: Model for Personhood-in-Relation," in Polkinghorne, *Trinity and an Entangled World*, 108.
20 Zizioulas, *Communion and Otherness*, 39.

21 John D. Zizioulas, *Being as Communion: Studies in Personhood and the Church* (London: Darton, Longman & Todd, 1985), 17, 40, 88, 46.

22 Mark A. McIntosh, *Mystical Theology: The Integrity of Spirituality and Theology* (Oxford: Blackwell, 1998), 194.

23 Ware, "Holy Trinity," 126.

24 McIntosh, *Mystical Theology*, 216.

25 Mark A. McIntosh, *Discernment and Truth: The Spirituality and Theology of Knowledge* (New York: Crossroads, 2004), 58.

26 Patricia A. Fox, *God as Communion: John Zizioulas, Elizabeth Johnson, and the Retrieval of the Triune God* (New York: Michael Glazier, 2001), 54.

Two: Postmodern Insights for Climate Change

1 Timothy Morton, *The Ecological Thought* (Cambridge, MA: Harvard University Press, 2010).

2 Karen Barad, "Posthumanist Performativity: Toward an Understanding of How Matter Comes to Matter," *Signs* 28, no. 3 (Spring 2003): 818.

3 Jane Bennett, *Vibrant Matter* (Durham, NC: Duke University Press, 2010), 122.

Three: Divine and Human Relational Ontology

1 Sallie McFague, *Super, Natural Christians: How We Should Love Nature* (Minneapolis: Fortress, 1997), 91–92.

2 Mary-Jane Rubenstein, *Strange Wonder: The Closure of Metaphysics and the Opening of Awe* (New York: Columbia University Press, 2008), 124, 23, 128.

3 Rubenstein, 195, 196.
4 Jean-Luc Nancy, *Adoration: The Deconstruction of Christianity II*, trans. John McKeane (New York: Fordham University Press, 2013), 1, 64, 62.
5 Nancy, 12, 15, 20.
6 Nancy, 18.
7 Nancy, 43.
8 Nancy, 53.
9 Nancy, 62.
10 Karmen MacKendrick, *Divine Enticement: Theological Seductions* (New York: Fordham University Press, 2013), 138.
11 MacKendrick, 30.
12 Augustine, *The Confessions of St. Augustine*, bks. 1–10, trans. F. J. Sheed (New York: Sheed & Ward, 1943), 176–77.
13 MacKendrick, *Divine Enticement*, 8.
14 MacKendrick, 7.
15 Stephanie Kaza, *The Attentive Heart: Conversations with Trees*, ill. Davis TeSelle (New York: Ballantine, 1993), 3.
16 Kaza, 7.

Four: God as Friend and We as Friends of the World

1 Nancey Murphy and George F. R. Ellis, *On the Moral Nature of the Universe* (Minneapolis: Fortress, 1996), 174.
2 C. S. Lewis, *The Four Loves: The Much Beloved Exploration of the Nature of Love* (New York: Harvest, 1960), 103.
3 Aristotle, *Nicomachean Ethics*, ed. and trans. John Warrington (London: J. M. Dent & Sons, 1963), 1155a.
4 Lewis, *Four Loves*, 124.

5 Sallie McFague, *Models of God: Theology for an Ecological, Nuclear Age* (Minneapolis: Fortress, 1987), 178.

6 Simone Weil, *Waiting for God*, trans. Emma Craufurd (New York: Harper & Row, 1951), 208.

7 Moltmann, *Crucified God*, 73.

8 Arthur C. McGill, *Sermons of Arthur C. McGill: Theological Fascinations*, ed. David Cain (Eugene, OR: Cascade, 2007), 1:100.

9 Arthur C. McGill, *The Uncertain Center: Essays of Arthur C. McGill*, ed. Kent Dunnington (Eugene, OR: Cascade, 2015), 149.

10 McGill, *Sermons*, 1:78.

11 Arthur C. McGill, *Death and Life: An American Theology*, ed. Charles A. Wilson and Per M. Anderson (Eugene, OR: Wipf & Stock, 1987), 75.

12 McGill, *Sermons*, 1:37.

13 For instance, see McGill, *Death and Life*, 81ff.

14 McGill, 26.

15 McGill, *Uncertain Center*, 136.

16 McGill, *Death and Life*, 86.

17 C. S. Lewis, *The Problem of Pain* (London: Fontana, 1957), 141.

18 Arthur C. McGill, *Dying unto Life: On New God, New Death, New Life*, ed. David Cain (Eugene, OR: Cascade, 2013), 63–64.

19 McGill, *Death and Life*, 51.

20 McGill, *Uncertain Center*, 112.

21 Arthur C. McGill, *Suffering: A Test of Theological Method*, with a foreword by Paul Ramsey and William F. May (Eugene, OR: Wipf & Stock, 1982), 53, 55.

22 McGill, *Sermons*, 1:141ff.

23 McGill, 1:23, 95.

24 McGill, 1:92, 94 (emphasis added).

25 McGill, *Dying unto Life*, 145.

26 McGill, *Suffering*, 60.

27 McGill, *Dying unto Life*, 141.

28 McGill, 70.

29 McGill, 69–70.

30 McGill, *Sermons*, 1:119.

31 Richard Kearney, *Anatheism (Returning to God after God)* (New York: Columbia University Press, 2011).

32 Richard Kearney, "Re-imagining God," in *Transcendence and Beyond: A Postmodern Inquiry*, ed. John D. Caputo and Michael J. Scanlon (Bloomington: Indiana University Press, 2007), 9.

33 Kearney, *Anatheism*, 80–81.

34 Kearney, 183.

35 Kearney, 63, 69.

36 Quoted from Dietrich Bonhoeffer in Kearney, 70.

37 Kearney, 76, 77.

38 Kearney, 91.

39 Kearney, 61.

40 Kearney, 85, 100.

41 Richard Kearney, "Desire of God," in *God, the Gift, and Postmodernism*, ed. John D. Caputo and Michael J. Scanlon (Bloomington: Indiana University Press, 1999), 112–45.

42 Kearney, "Re-imagining God," 62–63.

Five: Christian Theology in View of Kenosis, Theosis, and Postmodernism

1 See Stephen Finlan and Vladimir Kharlamov, ed., introduction to *Theosis*.

2   McIntosh, *Discernment and Truth*, 20.

3   Richard, *Kenotic Christology*, 261, 268.

4   Finch, "Irenaeus," 86.

5   McIntosh, *Discernment and Truth*, 6.

6   Pierre Teilhard de Chardin, *The Divine Milieu: An Essay on the Interior Life* (New York: Harper & Bros., 1960), 62.

7   Gorman, *Inhabiting the Cruciform God*, 34.

8   Gorman, 163.

9   Argyris Nicolaidis, "Relational Nature," in Polkinghorne, *Trinity and an Entangled World*, 99, 106, 101.

10 Zizioulas, *Communion and Otherness*, 5–6.

11 Richard, *Kenotic Christology*, 233.

12 John Caputo, *The Insistence of God: A Theology of Perhaps* (Bloomington: Indiana University Press, 2013), 52.

13 Caputo, 52, 237.

14 Richard, *Kenotic Christology*, 233.

15 As quoted in McFague, *Blessed Are the Consumers*, 64.

16 Barry Lopez, *Arctic Dreams: Imagination and Desire in a Northern Landscape* (New York: Bantam, 1987), 370.

Index